NEW EDITION

BUSINESS OBJECTIVES

TEACHER'S BOOK

Anna Phillips
Terry Phillips

Oxford University Press

Oxford University Press
Great Clarendon Street, Oxford OX2 6DP

Oxford New York
Athens Aukland Bankok Bogota Bombay
Buenos Aires Calcutta Cape Town Dar es Salaam
Delhi Florence Hong Kong Istanbul Karachi
Kuala Lumpur Madras Madrid Melbourne
Mexico City Nairobi Paris Singapore
Tapei Tokyo Toronto Warsaw
and associated companies in
Berlin Ibadan

Oxford and *Oxford English*
are trade marks of
Oxford University Press

ISBN 0 19 451393 9

© Oxford University Press

First published 1996
Third impression 1997

Printed by Progressive Printing (UK) Ltd., Essex

Photocopying

Acknowledgements

*The author and publisher would like to thank the following for
permission to use adapted material and/or to reproduce copy-
right material:*

Apple Macintosh, specifications of the Performa 6200 system;
BASF UK, information about the company from a leaflet, *Facts
and Figures*; BP, London, information from an article in the
Independent on Sunday 1995; The *European* newspaper,
information adapted from an article, 1995; the *Guardian*
newspaper, extract from an article on the Internet, 1996.

Design by Sarah Tyzack

Progress Tests by Pam Murphy and Vicki Hollett

Contents

Introduction

Using Business Objectives

Business Objectives is designed for groups of low intermediate learners. The book can also be used as a revision course.

Business Objectives can be used in two ways.

1   As a continuous course, to be used from start to finish. *Business Objectives* starts with simpler structures and vocabulary, and progresses quite rapidly to more complex language. Using the book in this way will enable students to gain a good basic working knowledge both of English grammar and of business English vocabulary.

2   As a resource to be dipped into. Each unit is free-standing. There is no storyline or background information to preclude the random use of individual activities. Using the book in a flexible manner will enable teachers to cater for the specific priorities of different groups. For example, engineers may be especially interested in Unit 4 (Exchanging Information) and Unit 14 (Company Visits): financial specialists may be more interested in Unit 9 (Describing Trends) and Unit 10 (Progress Updates).

Format of units

All fifteen units follow a broadly similar format.

PRESENTATION

Key language points are often presented in the form of a listening text. The material is generally exploited in the following ways:

*   *Listening for content.* The teacher plays the taped conversations right through. A task-based activity helps students follow the gist of the conversation and pick out specific points of information.

*   *Listening for language.* In this phase the focus shifts to the forms of the language. The dialogue is replayed, while students complete exercises designed to highlight specific words and phrases.

LANGUAGE WORK

This section provides controlled practice of the target language in each unit. Some written exercises are included, but the emphasis is on oral practice. Many of these activities involve work in pairs and small groups. This has the advantage of maximizing the amount of practice that students get. Students who have not experienced this type of practice before may be worried about making mistakes, and may require reassurance. Monitor the pair and small group work closely and encourage students to ask for help when necessary.

SKILLS WORK

This section includes a speaking task, along with one or more reading, writing, or listening tasks.

The speaking tasks here represent the culminating challenge of the unit. They are generally freer than the speaking practice in the language work section. They are also more demanding: students will need to draw on all their linguistic resources, rather than on language just learnt. It is important that students do not feel they have failed if they make linguistic mistakes in these activities. Success here should be judged on communicative effectiveness rather than structural accuracy.

It is often a good idea to give your students time to prepare these speaking activities. You may also wish to allow plenty of time at the end for a thorough debriefing, enabling any problems encountered to be aired, good language and communication practice to be praised, and poor performance identified and corrected.

The reading and listening texts in this section are accompanied by task-based comprehension activities, plus discussion and/or vocabulary work. The texts are generally longer and more difficult than elsewhere. Students may encounter new language items not previously practised. At this stage, however, a passive knowledge is all that is required. Complicated explanations should not be necessary.

Practice is also provided in writing business letters, reports, and fax messages. Managers who enjoy plenty of secretarial help may prefer to miss out these activities.

> In this Teacher's Book, the answers to exercises are easily located in shaded boxes. The surrounding notes provide more detailed help with some exercises as well as notes on aspects of the language.

Appendices

Information Files

Some activities require pairs of students to exchange different sets of information. In these cases, role-play notes for one member of each pair are provided in numbered files at the back of the Student's Book.

Grammar notes

Notes on the grammatical structures and uses covered in the course, and a list of irregular verbs, are located at the back of the Student's Book. You may wish to draw students' attention to this reference source at the beginning of the course.

Tapescripts

In the new edition, tapescripts are continuously numbered both in the Student's Book, using the cassette symbol, and on the tape itself.

Glossary

The Student's Book also includes a glossary with explanations in English. Students at this level are likely to be reliant on bilingual dictionaries, and the glossary may be employed as a first step towards using an English-English dictionary.

Teaching Business English

The debate about how much specialist knowledge is necessary to teach English for Specific Purposes is an old one that will continue well into the future. *Business Objectives* has been designed to meet the practical needs of the numerous business English teachers whose specialist knowledge and direct experience of the business world is not extensive. Two elements in particular have shaped its approach:

- Making the most of authentic materials. Documentation from real firms has been used to ensure business authenticity and relevance.

- Making the most of the students' professional expertise. Many activities involve students in relating and discussing their own business experiences to ensure they contribute directly to the course content. This may mean that the teacher will not always be in a position to supply the specialist terms the students need. This should not be a major problem provided you make clear your limitations at the start of the course. On balance, the benefits of

encouraging students to discuss their 'real-life' business experiences far outweigh any drawbacks.

The tasks in this course will often involve students in expressing their own ideas and opinions and giving accounts of events in their own workplaces. In this way the activity and language employed will relate to the students' individual needs and experience. For teachers using the course with students who have not yet embarked on their careers, guidance and alternative activities are included in this teacher's book.

Both the teacher and the student have expertise in their own field, the teacher in English and the student in business. The resulting exchange of knowledge is extremely positive - good for students because it allows real communication, and good for teachers who will develop a growing - if indirect - understanding of the business world.

New edition

This is the new edition of the Business Objectives course. Teachers familiar with the first edition may wish to note the following changes.

- Numbered tapescripts are now available at the back of the Student's Book.

- Each unit contains practice in a feature of English pronunciation.

- There are now 15 enlarged units.

- Vocabulary work is more systematic and is now listed in the Student's Book index.

- There are now learner training activities.

- **PX** This Teacher's Book has been improved and now contains optional activities for pre-experience students. These are all indicated by the above symbol.

Progress tests

Five photocopiable progress tests are now included in this edition of the Teacher's Book. Each test covers three consecutive units of the course and lasts around forty-five minutes depending on the level and ability of your students.

Suggested marks for each exercise appear at the top right of each one. The marks total 100 for each test. You could point this out to your students so that they can allot the appropriate time and effort.

PRESENTATION

> **Optional equipment and materials**
>
> Cards with the names of local companies on for Activity 1

At the start of the course draw students' attention to the 'objectives' and 'tasks' that introduce each unit so that they are aware of the goals of each unit as you start out.

1 Introduce yourself in the way shown in the Student's Book as a model for the activity. Get the statements on the board.

With large classes get students out of their seats to mingle and introduce themselves to each other. When they have sat down again, see how much they can remember about the other students in the class, for example, *What's his name? Who does he work for?*

With students from the same company, get them to give the name of their department rather than the company, for example, *I work in …*

As a game, try to remember companies and departments yourself and get the students to correct you.

PX These students will not be able to say *I work for …*

If the whole class is pre-experience, hand out cards with the names of local companies on. Otherwise let pre-experience students say *I'm a student.*

2 Exploit the visuals. Direct students' attention to the clothes that the people are wearing and check where the people are.

1 Check the convention of shaking hands in British and American culture. Teach or elicit that we shake hands the first time we meet someone.

2 Check the convention of kissing on the cheek or both cheeks in British and American culture. Teach or elicit that men never kiss each other and sometimes kiss women if they know them well; women sometimes kiss each other, when they are good friends.

Ask the questions. Don't confirm or deny ideas for Question 2 at this point.

> **1** a – informal; b and c – formal
> **2** no answers at this point

3 ⊡ Check that students understand what to do. (Do this throughout the course.)

Play each conversation once, then let students compare their answers in pairs. Do not confirm or correct yet. Play all three conversations again if the students are obviously having difficulty.

> **1** Picture b
> **2** Picture c
> **3** Picture a

4 🔲 Give students a few moments to read the sentences and think about what is missing. Make sure students realize there is one word for each underline.

Play Conversation 1a again.

Let students compare answers in pairs.

Ask students to find the tapescript on page 181.

Play the cassette again so that students can listen and follow the script.

(This may seem excessive but at this point ear training is absolutely vital. Students must begin to relate the sound and sight of words and phrases to help them establish word boundaries when they are listening to the stream of speech.)

Louise:	may I introduce this is
Mr Velázquez:	How do you do?
Peter:	How do you do?
Louise:	responsible for

5 ☐ᵇ This is best done as pairwork. Put some process language on the board to assist students in the discussion:

I think this one is first because …
No, I think it's this one because …
I (don't) think this one is next because …

Give plenty of time for students to complete the activity.

Play conversation 1b again straight through, **or**, stop after each sentence and ask students who speaks next and what s/he says, then play the next sentence to check.

Ask students to find the tapescript on page 181.

Play the cassette again so that students can listen and follow the script.

| 3 6 I 7 4 2 5 |

6 ☐ᶜ As before, give students time to read the instructions and the sentences for correction.

(Throughout the course, always give plenty of time to setting up each activity and, if students have to read and listen at the same time, give them time to read through once **before** listening.)

Play conversation 1c again straight through.

Students work on their own, then compare in pairs.

Check answers. If students are struggling, refer to the tapescript on page 181 and play the cassette again so that students can listen and follow the script.

I	It's the evening.
2	Bob and Liz work together.
3	Luigi is in the chemicals business.

Put students into threes to practise all three introductions.

7 Teach or elicit some of the language from the lesson so far, then refer students to the activity.

Go through the first situation with a good student as an example, then put students in pairs to continue. Monitor, but try not to interrupt or correct during the activity. Draw attention to the coloured boxes containing phrases they will find

useful. Highlight general points of difficulty at the end.

8 Teach or elicit the ideas behind these greeting and parting expressions.

The way people divide up the day depends on the language they speak. There are also differences between languages about whether greetings can also be used as partings.

Here is the way British and Americans divide up the day, and which expressions they use when greeting someone or parting from them.

	6am – noon	noon – 6pm	after 6pm
Greeting	Good morning	Good afternoon	Good evening
Parting	Goodbye	Goodbye	Goodbye or Goodnight

LANGUAGE WORK

> **Optional equipment and materials**
> For pre-experience students – business cards for Describing Jobs 2

Kᴇʏ ʟᴀɴɢᴜᴀɢᴇ ᴘᴏɪɴᴛs

Articles: The use of definite and indefinite articles and the rules governing the omission of articles change from language to language. Students must become sensitive to when articles are used and which article is used in English.

In this section the following points are covered.

Indefinite article for the job you do, unless you are the only one with that title. Compare: *I'm a finance director* with *I'm the Finance Director.*

No article for company names or abstract nouns or plural countables. *I'm in marketing* or *chemicals. I'm responsible for production.*

Also note that in English the indefinite article is *a* before consonants and consonant sounds and *an* before vowels and vowel sounds. It is not directly connected with the noun so if an adjective precedes the noun, this will affect the form of the article.

7

I'm an engineer – I'm an electrical engineer – I'm a civil engineer.

Present Simple: Use of the verb *to be* and other verbs in the Present Simple.

Make sure students are using final *s* and *does* for third person singular.

Getting information

1 Work through the first card, asking and getting answers to the questions.

Get answers on the board. Highlight key grammar points in the answers.

> Her name's Birgitte Svensson.
> She's Swedish.
> She works for Skanesbanken.
> She works in Stockholm.
> She's the Deputy Managing Director.

Get students to ask and answer questions about the other people in pairs.

2 As Student's Book.

3 Refer students back to the question words in the last activity. Then set activity.

Individual activity then check through pairwork.

As an extra activity, give each answer, and ask students to make questions.

To find out about IPQ's newest product.
Why are you here?

This is a good lead in to Activity 4.

> Why
> What
> How
> Who
> Which – notice that *which* is used when there is a limited number of options.
> When
> Where

4 With a weak class, go through the whole exercise with the class together answering orally, then set as written activity. Otherwise do two or three as examples, then set for individual written work.

> 1 How do you do?
> 2 What's your name?
> 3 How do you spell José?
> 4 What nationality are you?
> 5 Are you married?
> 6 Who do you work for?
> 7 What do they do?
> 8 Which department do you work in?
> 9 What do you do?
> 10 Which languages do you speak?

5 As Student's Book.

PX If the whole class is pre-experience, get students to write the questions to you.

If some students in the group work, get pre-experience students to write questions for them. Then work in groups to ask the questions with at least one non-pre-experience student in each group.

Describing jobs

1 Give students time to look at the table. Depending on their culture, students might like to copy the table into their notebooks. Ask students how they say these things in their own languages, concentrating on article usage. With a monolingual class, contrast. Explain that the table will help them complete the activity below.

Individual activity, then students compare in pairs.

> in   for   a   for   in   an

2

Encourage students to give exact information here, even if you struggle to work out exactly what the jobs and work areas are.

PX Give out business cards for students to role-play the jobs, **or** ask students to say what they would like to be or will be in a year's time.

3 Do the first question with the class.

8

> Executive managers: 5
> Divisions: 6

Go through the examples on page 11 and get the answers. Then do a few more exchanges following the same model with the whole class, before putting students in pairs to complete.

> Questions and answers depend on the students. See Student's Book, page 11 for model questions.

The divisions report directly to the President. Also: *If A reports to B, A is also responsible to B.*

If B is in charge of production, he is also responsible for production.

4 Don't worry too much about the form of the students' responses. The structures are dealt with more fully in the next section.

PX Ask each student to imagine s/he is one of the people on the organigram on page 10 of the Student's Book, then set the task.

Commuters

1 Teach or elicit the word *commuter*.

Exploit the visuals, but be careful! If you ask students *What is X doing?* make sure you reset the idea that these people do these things every day and that therefore in many cases the Present Simple would be more appropriate.

Work through the example with the whole class, then set the others for pairwork.

> ***Matthew Long***
> Where does he work?
> Where does he live?
> How does he travel to work?
> How long does it take him?
> How far is it?
> What does he do during the journey?
>
> ***Daisule and Hideo Nakajima***
> Where do they work?
> Where do they live?
> How do they travel to work?
> How long does the journey take?
> What do they do during the journey?

2 As Student's Book.

> ***Possible questions to ask:***
> Where do you work?
> Where do you live?
> How do you travel to work?
> How far is it?
> What time do you leave home?
> What do you do on the journey?

PX Ask a partner about their journey to college or school.

Countries and nationalities

1 Get the example on to the board and point out the connection between the nationality and the country.

Do the activity orally without preamble and teach or elicit the nationalities and countries as you go through. Then repeat with students working in pairs. See chart.

> 1   Japan, Japanese
> 2   The USA, American
> 3   Italy, Italian
> 4   Sweden, Swedish
> 5   Norway, Norwegian
> 6   France, French
> 7   Britain, British
> 8   Switzerland, Swiss
> 9   Germany, German
> 10 The Netherlands (Holland), Dutch

2 As Student's Book – individual then pairwork checking. Give feedback then practise the pronunciation and stress pattern of each word, especially stress shift: *Italy – Italian.*

9

3 As Student's Book. The origins of some of the stamps may not be obvious.

The stamps/envelopes are from:
Argentina - Argentinian
Brazil - Brazilian
France - French
Germany - German (Deutschland)
Hungary - Hungarian (Magyar Posta)
Italy - Italian
Japan - Japanese (Nippon)
Malaysia - Malay(sian)
Russia - Russian
Spain - Spanish (España)
Taiwan - Taiwanese
Thailand - Thai
Turkey - Turkish

PX Ask students if they know of any imports from each of these countries. For example, 'We import Brazilian coffee.'

Personality profile

1 Remember this is an information gap activity so do not confirm or correct any ideas or suggestions. You can encourage crazy way-out answers.

2 Pairwork. Set up the information gap carefully. (This type of activity recurs throughout the course.) Perhaps work with two students at the front of the class to show exactly what they must each do.

As a variation on checking feedback, let the student who has written the answers refer to File 1 page 158 and compare what s/he wrote with the correct version and discuss any problems or mistakes and why they occurred.

1	Where does he come from?	Taiwan
2	Where does he live?	Hong Kong
3	How old is he?	42
4	What kind of business is he in?	Distribution
5	What does he do in his spare time?	Rock music
6	How many cars has he got?	10
7	What unusual machine does he have in his mini?	Karaoke
8	What does George hate?	Numbers
9	What else does he hate?	Ties

Check overall comprehension with a 'Many a slip' game. You read the text, Students' Books closed, but make mistakes with the content – not the grammar, for example: *George Wong comes from Hong Kong but lives in Taiwan ..., He's 14 years of age, very successful and he loves his wife.* The students have to correct you.

Pronunciation

1 ☐₂ Show students how to mark the stress – with underlining. For example, *inter**na**tional.* This is the most useful way for recording vocabulary in their notebooks.

You could also show students how to mark the stress with a vertical stroke in front of the stressed syllable. For example, *inter'national.* This is useful for self-access checking in dictionaries.

Give students time to mark the stress themselves, then play the words on the cassette for checking.

Finally get the correct version on the board.

a	construction
b	engineer
c	headquarters
d	financial
e	European
f	responsible
g	responsibilities
h	nationality

2 As Student's Book.

SKILLS WORK

> **Optional equipment and materials**
>
> Coins and OHT of games board if possible for Speaking 1
>
> Business cards for pre-experience students for Writing

Speaking 1

Pairwork or groups of three. Show students how to play the game – using a coin and an OHT of the board if possible. Or desmonstrate with 2 students.

Teach or elicit *coin*, *heads*, *tails* and the expressions: *It's your turn/go. Is it my turn/go?*

Show students how to judge the answers of their partner or group. Monitor but do not interrupt. Deal with any general problems at the end.

Writing

This could be done as homework or classwork.

As homework: point out the relationship between the reading passage and writing activity and check that students understand exactly what they must do.

As classwork: get students to find, underline and annotate each piece of information: *My name is Derek Stirling – name*; *I'm Scottish – nationality*, etc.

Get the list of information headings on the board. Ask students to make notes about themselves in the same order. Ask students to write a paragraph about themselves from the notes.

This task and Speaking 2 should provide you with useful biographical information. Make notes of any interesting information to help you target activities in later units.

PX Students can work with business cards as previously, or create their own imaginary answer

Speaking 2

Pairwork. This is a learner-training activity designed to assist learners in organizing and taking charge of their own learning.

Direct students' attention to the illustration at the bottom of page 15. Ask them what materials and equipment they can see that could help them learn English. They should be able to find:

a personal stereo (Walkman)
a computer
a satellite dish
a video recorder
a telephone
a newspaper
stationery items: pen, pencil, Post-it notes, liquid paper and so on.

Discuss how these things might be useful.

2 Telephoning

PRESENTATION

> **Optional equipment and materials**
>
> Copies of forms for Activity 1

1 ⬜ Give students time to look closely at the two forms and check comprehension of what the forms contain. The first is a sales prospect form, and the second is an order form.

Teach or elicit: *sales prospect, order request, customer.*

Ask students when Galaxy Computer Supplies use each form.

Refer students back to the forms and ask them to think about the questions that might be asked and the way they might be answered. This is essential preparation for the listening.

Play each conversation straight through once.

If students are struggling, play the conversations again, pausing at key points to give time for writing.

> *First conversation*
>
> | | |
> |---|---|
> | **Name:** | José Rosales |
> | **Company:** | EVP |
> | **Fax:** | 91 430 6687 |
> | **Area of Interest:** | BZ 11 |
> | **Action necessary:** | send quote |

> *Second conversation*
>
> | | |
> |---|---|
> | **Contact name:** | Christophe Terrien |
> | **Company:** | RGF |
> | **Quantity:** | 6 units |
> | **Ref. No. :** | 76905A/K |
> | **Order received:** | by phone |

2 ⬜ Give students time to read the questions for Conversation 3a.

Play the conversation again. If necessary, play it again while students follow in the tapescript on page 181.

> **a** Because the lines are busy.
> **b** She promises to work out the price and fax a quotation through immediately.

Repeat this procedure for Conversation 3b.

> **c** Do you have them in stock?
> **d** Confirm the order in writing.

3 As Student's Book.

With exercises in two columns like this one, the activity can be fully exploited by following this procedure:

1 Set matching activity.

2 Give students time to compare in pairs.

3 Ask students to cover top half and remember bottom half. Then they can switch around.

> | | | | | | |
> |---|---|---|---|---|---|
> | 1 | f | 5 | c | 9 | e |
> | 2 | i | 6 | d | 10 | h |
> | 3 | a | 7 | b | | |
> | 4 | g | 8 | j | | |

In large classes, write expressions on cards, give one to each student and ask them to find a partner.

LANGUAGE WORK

> **Optional equipment and materials**
>
> Copies of chart for pronunciation of letters of the alphabet for Pronunciation 2
>
> OHT of requests network for Requests 2

Starting calls

1 ☐4 Refer students to the table – let them copy it into their notebooks if appropriate. Remind them that the table will help with the following activity.

Individual then pairwork checking. Point out to students that in these conversations they can fit more than one word in each space. Do not confirm or correct yet.

Play the cassette for final checking.

Point out how *this* / *that* can be used for introducing yourself and asking about the other person on the telephone.

> 1 Could I speak to
> 2 I'd like to speak to / Speaking
> 3 Extension / Is that / It is

Pronunciation

1 ☐5a Ask students to look at the chart below and practise pronouncing the letters.

2 Give out copies of the blank chart below.

3 ☐5b As Student's Book. Play the cassette several times if necessary.

> 1 HISKETT
> 2 LJUBLJANA
> 3 GYÖR
> 4 CAIPIRINHA
> 5 DHANIN SERIBURI

4 Pairwork. As Student's Book. Problems could arise with the dictation or the hearing of letters. Encourage students to try to deduce how mistakes happened.

Abbreviations are often turned into words if they have consonant vowel consonant structure: *ohpeck / jal*. But some which do follow this pattern are not pronounced as words, for example, *f o b*.

If you identify particular problems for some or all of your students, repeat pronunciation practice of those letters. All the vowels and the consonants R, H, G, J, S, X, often cause particular problems.

Transferring information

1 and **2** Pairwork. Get students to identify the differences between British and American English.

0: AmE = *zero*; BrE = *oh*.
66: AmE = *six six*; BrE = *double six*

Then proceed as in the Student's Book. Encourage students to deduce how mistakes happen.

In the UK telephone numbers are often pronounced in groups of three, unlike many countries where they are grouped in pairs.

A	B	C	D	E	F	G	H	I	J	K	L	M	N	O	P	Q	R	S	T	U	V	W	X	Y	Z
	1			2				3				4				5				6			7		
	A			B				F				I								Q					

PX Get students to exchange only home numbers.

With weaker students, give further practice by dictating some numbers twice – the second time with differences. Can they spot the differences?

3 Silence fillers are important elements of real conversation. Without them there can be embarrassing silences and/or a feeling that the other person does not understand or follow what you are saying.

Refer students to the table which is preparation for the activity which follows.

Demonstrate the first message-giving task with a good student, then set whole activity for pairwork.

With weaker classes, dictate the messages again, making mistakes for students to correct.

Deciding what to do

1 Point out that 'll is a contraction of *will* which has many uses – one is to introduce a solution to a problem or a new idea, which is practised here.

Go through the first two problems and their solutions, then set for pairwork. Alternatively, as a change of pace, set this activity for writing, even though this is clearly a spoken form.

With a strong class, get students to cover the words in brackets and ask them to think of their own solutions.

> ***Possible answers***
> **2** I'll come back later.
> **3** I'll order some.
> **4** I'll hire a translator.
> **5** I'll find another supplier.
> **6** I'll give you a lift.
> **7** I'll send them a fax.
> **8** I'll get a glass of water.

2 Refer students to the cartoons and ask them to match each cartoon with one of the reasons.

Encourage students to preface any ideas with *I'm afraid* ... Make sure students are not saying *I'm afraid but* ... .

> **1** c   **2** d   **3** e   **4** a   **5** b

3 As Student's Book except with weak classes. In this case, you will have to build up the conversations carefully with them, perhaps getting them on the board, before putting students in pairs to practise.

Requests

1 Teach or elicit phrases for politely asking people to do something.

Practise the pronunciation especially the /dʒ/ sound where *d* meets *y*.

Point out that all three have the same meaning and grammar but *Can you* ... is less formal. *Could you* ... and *would you* ... are better in situations where we don't know the person very well.

Do the activity with the whole class.

> ***Possible answers***
> **a** Could you speak up / louder please?
> **b** Could you repeat that please?
> **c** Could you speak more slowly / slow down please?
> **d** Could you spell that please?
> **e** Could you transfer me to the Finance Department?

2 Work your way through the visual, using an OHT if possible, and taking the part of the person making the request with one or two of the following situations suggested in the Student's Book.

This exercise should naturally draw out some refusals! Point out that refusals are normally introduced by an apology and followed by a reason: *I'm afraid I can't because* ... . Pairwork.

Vocabulary note: *Borrow* and *lend* are often confused. Show that you *borrow* **from** and *lend* **to** someone. Point out that both are temporary. Borrowing is like taking and lending is like giving.

3 Point out that the expressions in the table are also requests, but requests for permission.

Again *can* is more informal; *could* is preferable. *May* is almost too polite for some situations. *Could* therefore is perhaps the most informal and the most versatile for students to learn to produce, with both *I* and *you*.

Pairwork. Monitor and get individual students to give their ideas at the end.

> ### Possible questions to ask
> 1 Can I use you phone?
> 2 Could I smoke in here?
> 3 Can I look at your copy of the production plan, please?
> 4 Could I copy a file from your computer?
> 5 Could/May I borrow your copy of the Economist?
> 6 Could/May I borrow your car?

4 This checks that students understand some key vocabulary items plus the function of the requesting phrases. Check *customer* and *supplier* carefully before starting. Pairwork.

> | | | | | | |
> |---|---|---|---|---|---|
> | 1 | C | 4 | C | 7 | C |
> | 2 | S | 5 | S | 8 | S |
> | 3 | S | 6 | C | | |

The second part of this activity may be very hard for weaker students. Let them write the conversation first.

5 As Student's Book

SKILLS WORK

> **Optional equipment and materials**
> OHTs of letters for Writing

Listening

1 6a Teach or elicit *answering machine*.

Point out that students only have to find the answers to the two questions.

Play the cassette several times if necessary until students confirm that they have the information.

At some point, but not until students have heard the cassette at least once, teach or elicit the meaning of *pager* – a device for leaving a message, i.e. you cannot talk to the person you wish to speak to directly.

> **a** London
> **b** Pager number 091 551 804

2 6b If you have done several 'Spot the mistake' exercises, go straight into this one. If not, work through the first one until the students spot the first mistake. Individual then pairwork checking. As before, be prepared to let students look at the tapescript during further listening if they are struggling.

> ### Mistakes are
> 1 Terry **not** Jerry
> 2 506211 **not** 50621
> 3 Thursday's **not** Tuesday's meeting
> 4 Call him Wednesday after 11 **not** tomorrow

3 6c As Student's Book

> 1 from Lorella Lazzari (spelling of Lorella might differ but surname should be correctly spelt)
> 2 2 -738 - 2541
> 3 She is confirming the arrangements for your visit to Milan. She will call again tomorrow

4 6d Make sure students understand about voice mail – an electronic message taking system.

> John Crosby Ext. 8241

5 6e Teach or elicit ☆ star and # hash keys. In AmE, the # key is called the 'pound' key but in BrE it is called the 'hash' key.

As always give students time to read before starting the cassette. Play several times – you could do this in real life anyway.

> a 6   c 7   e #
> b 4   d 2

Speaking

If this is the first time your students have done this kind of activity, work through a complete example with two good students sitting at the front of the class. Then put students in pairs. Monitor. Get good pairs to demonstrate at the end of the activity. These two activities lead into the writing activity.

Writing

1 Try to ensure that you give class time for this as it is more effective as pairwork than homework.

> Dear Ms Thatcher
> With reference to...
> I am writing to...
> I would be grateful if you could...
> Thank you for your help.
> Yours sincerely,

2 To make the most of the phrases in Activity 2, make sure students study the expressions on page 26 before completing the two letters.

1 Get students to label expressions in the example letter by using the headings from Activity 2.

2 Ask students to complete the letters using appropriate phrases. There are three forms of address for women: *Mrs* – married; *Miss* – unmarried; *Ms* (pronounced /mɪz/ – marital status not disclosed).

> *Possible answers*
>
> **Letter 1**
> 1 With reference to …
> 2 I'm writing to apologize …
> 3 Unfortunately …
> 4 I am enclosing …
> 5 Please contact us again if we can help in any way.
> 6 Yours sincerely …
>
> **Letter 2**
> 1 Thank you for …
> 2 I am writing …
> 3 I would be delighted to …
> 4 Could you possibly …
> 5 I look forward to hearing from you soon …
> 6 Best wishes …

3 Companies

PRESENTATION

> **Optional equipment and materials**
> OHT of table for Activities 2, 3, and 4

1 Set this activity as a warm-up. Do not confirm or correct students' suggestions yet.

2 [7] Play the three sections once.

Remember! This is a global listening activity. Do not ask for any information except which company each speaker is talking about.

3 [7a] As Student's Book. Students can fill in the form in the Student's Book, or the answers could be organized as a table which you can construct on the board, adding information after each listening, as shown below.

4 [7b] As Student's Book.

[PX] There is a lot of vocabulary in these three listening sections. With pre-experience students,

consider doing a 'reverse dictionary' vocabulary check. For this you give the definition and students tell you the word:
People who work for a company: employees.
Places that planes travel to: destinations.

5 [7c] As Student's Book

LANGUAGE WORK

KEY LANGUAGE POINT: There is no difference in meaning between *has* and *has got*. Both can indicate possession in a broad sense. *Has got* is common in spoken BrE. But questions and negatives are formed differently.

Company profiles

Ask students to read the two conversations in pairs and compare them. Focus attention on the meaning first, then the form. Are they both talking about possession? Do they have the same form?

	Companies	Products & Services	Current projects / activities	Numbers
1	Philips	Electrical products	Expanding activities in China Developing joint ventures in China	250,000 employees 120 subsidiaries 31,626 m ECU (turnover) 1m products
2	Japan Airways	International and domestic flights	Installing Future Aircraft Navigation Systems in aircraft (FANS) Improving communications and reducing air traffic congestion by using satellite links	30 m passengers p.a. 41 destinations 25 countries 48 routes 21 cities
3	IBM	Advanced information processing products Micro electronics Data storage Communications	Throwing out bureaucracy Developing a new company culture Introducing new systems	$62 billion turnover 215,000 employees

We do not normally mix up the two forms in the same part of a conversation. So if you ask someone a question with *has got* they will reply with the same form. Remind students of this before they do the speaking practice activity.

Exploit the visual and deal with some of the new vocabulary, but do not spend too long on this – the main point, at this stage, is the structure.

Set up pairwork. Monitor and give feedback on any general difficulties.

Students can ask and answer about their own companies.

Facilities

KEY LANGUAGE POINT: *There is* or *There are* are used to introduce new topics or items.

It is or *They are* are used to give extra information about a known topic or item. The information is most often in the form of an adjective but can be a noun. Therefore:

There is / are … often refer forwards, and *It is / They are …* often refer backwards: *There is a computer in the office. It is very modern. It is a DX2-66.*

Refer students to Grammar Note on page 31 of Student's Book.

1 As Student's Book.

2 As Student's Book.

> **Possible sentences**
> It's dark.
> There's a map.
> There are some photographs.
> It isn't similar to my office.
> There isn't a window.
> There aren't any plants.

3 Teach or elicit at least the following words before setting activity: *disabled, lift, smoker, crèche.* Pairwork.

PX Ask students to think about the college or school where they are studying – either your own or the main one if they are full-time students in another institute.

Organizations

Give students time to study the diagram and check comprehension by asking a few simple questions such as, *How many departments are there? Which department is maintenance in?*

Give students plenty of time for this activity. Some of the definitions are relatively easy, others more difficult. Encourage students to do the ones they can do easily first, then go back and try to work out the others.

a	packaging	**i**	personnel
b	advertising	**j**	production
c	wages and salaries	**k**	customer accounts
d	buying	**l**	after-sales service
e	sales	**m**	distribution
f	marketing	**n**	quality
g	maintenance	**o**	financial services
h	training		

Departments are usually organized by activity or tasks performed: Marketing, Production. Divisions often relate to a geographical area or product line: North America, Plastics.

Pronunciation

1 [8a] As Student's Book. Let students listen several times to develop awareness of the three endings.

2 [8b] As Student's Book.

> The following words are pronounced with /ɪz/:
> *places, purchases, services, arranges, invoices, dispatches, organizes.*

Brighter students might like to work out why. The answer: /ɪz/ added to words that end with /s/, /z /, /dz/, or /tʃ/ sounds.

18

Current activities

KEY LANGUAGE POINT: The contrast is between what a company **does** – its area of business – and what it is **doing** – its current activity. Remind students of the contrast through the Grammar Note on page 33. Note also that we use the Present Continuous for actions happening around the present time, not just for things physically occurring at the moment of speaking.

1 Teach or elicit at least the following: *expand*, *life cycle*, *IT – information technology*, *develop*.

Remind students about making the verb *to be* agree in number – *is/are*.

b	is developing	**f**	am calling
c	are staying	**g**	are getting
d	is waiting	**h**	is going
e	are building	**i**	is spending

2 As Student's Book. Pairwork

PX Ask students to talk about what is happening in the country or area at the moment:

Who is building new premises?
Which companies are expanding?
Are any new products coming onto the market?

… and what is happening in the school or college:

Are they changing any of the courses?
Are they improving any of the facilities?
Are they preparing for any exams?

Company strengths

1 This could turn into an interesting discussion.

PX Ask students, in groups, to think about a large local company. Which of these statements about the company would make them buy its products?

2 Ask students to look at page 35 and do exercise. Encourage students to give their immediate responses, then to go on and really search for the answers. Ideally, you should not need to go through the answers at all if you really push students to keep looking.

a	T	**c**	T	**e**	T
b	F	**d**	T	**f**	F

3 As Student's Book.

PX Do further work on the McDonald's text. Get students to find the company's strengths and put them on the board. Students can close their books and explain each strength in their own words.

Strengths:

- Value
- Advertising
- Training
- Face to face meetings
- Close relationships with suppliers
- Cultural sensitivity
- Customer service

SKILLS WORK

Listening 9

Ask students what they know – if anything – about BICC. Encourage them to guess (if they know nothing) by looking at the organigram and pictures. Ask the students to guess what is missing from each space.

Play the cassette once straight through, without any activity, just to get the students used to the voice.

Set the activity and play the cassette again.

As before, if students are struggling, after playing the cassette several times, let students read the tapescript whilst they listen and check their ideas.

1	Four billion pounds	**5**	£595m
2	Construction	**6**	North America
3	fibre optic	**7**	Asia-Pacific
4	£1183		

Speaking

1 As Student's Book.

2 Give plenty of class time for this. If there is time and interest, get students to prepare visuals to support their presentations.

PX If your students are imaginative, they could work in groups to invent companies – perhaps very futuristic ones – and make up a presentation. They could then take it in turns to give the presentation. As above, they could make visuals if there is time and interest. Alternatively they could look through company annual reports, extracting the information they need to give the presentation.

PRESENTATION

Optional equipment and materials

Aerosol can

Remote control

Ring-pull can

Something with a bar code for Activity 1

---

1 Ask students to cover the words in the box and just look at the pictures. Give them a few moments to try to think of the names of the items. Do not confirm or correct yet.

Let students uncover the words and complete the activity. Do not start explaining any of the words.

Individual then pairwork checking.

Practise saying the new vocabulary.

2 ▢10 Write the word INVENTION on the board and explain that all the items are inventions. Ask for an example of a recent invention – in their particular field if the students are working, in general if they are pre-experience.

Ask students if they know anything about these inventions, asking particularly *When, Who, How,* or *Why* questions. Do not confirm or correct yet. It does not matter if they don't know anything yet. This is preparation for the listening activity.

Set the activity. Ask them to close their books so they don't 'read along' for this part.

Play the cassette straight through. Try to prevent students talking at this stage. Explain it is an individual activity.

Pairwork checking. Play again straight through if there is confusion.

1	ring-pull opener	4	pinball machine
2	remote control	5	barcode
3	aerosol can		

3 ▢10a This activity is mainly for training the ear and establishing word boundaries. Set the question after listening.

was designed: originally, in the past
is designed: now, part of the product description = purpose

4 ▢10b

were

5 ▢10c

1	were	4	was
2	was	5	was
3	were	6	were

6 ▢10d

wasn't   weren't

7 ▢10e

1	wasn't	5	weren't
2	was	6	were
3	was	7	were
4	wasn't	8	weren't

Although the texts are quite complex, the task is relatively easy in each case.

For weaker students: if you have time, you can exploit the texts further. For example:

1 students close their books again – you quote sentences or phrases from the descriptions and the students have to say which product description each one comes from.

2 students make a table putting the inventions in chronological order.

3 students find and underline adjectives – in preparation for the Language Work.

4 students say what particular adjectives refer to for example, circular – the early bar codes; not sophisticated – the early pinball machines.

LANGUAGE WORK

Optional equipment and materials

Adjective / noun matrix for Description 2

Advertising leaflets from two competing products in the local market for Description 5

As many phones (real or dummy) as possible for Size and Dimension 2

Description

1 If this is a new lesson, remind students of some of the adjectives in the Presentation section.

Refer students to the word box on page 40. Practise pronouncing the words, and get students to mark the stress in multi-syllable words.

2 As Student's Book.

---

1 fast, expensive, short, large, old-fashioned, boring, wonderful

2 (Note use of prefixes or suffixes to give opposite meaning) uncomfortable, inefficient, unfriendly, inexperienced, useless.

3 Answers depend on the students.

For 3, ask students to construct a matrix (this is optional) with the adjectives down the side and the nouns from the captions across the top – or give out one prepared in advance – see table below.

	weather	hotels	journeys	lessons	people	restaurants
cold	√		√			√
old-fashioned		√		√	√	√
expensive						
(in)efficient						
(un)friendly						
crowded						
windy						
wonderful						
boring						
five-star						
busy						
useless						
short						
tiring						
inexperienced						
informative						
fast						
entertaining						
large						
uncomfortable						

Point out that *in–* at the beginning of a word does not always have a negative meaning, for example, informative. With a strong class, encourage students to give you adjectives with less positive connotations with these prefixes and suffixes, and with others, for example, *im-, il-, ir-.*

3 1 Pairwork. Do the first two questions with the students and elicit possible answers. Emphasize that the course was excellent, therefore all the adjectives must have positive connotations.

Q: *What was ... like?* A: *It was ... (not It was like ...)*

2 As 1 above but emphasize the holiday was terrible so all the adjectives must have negative connotations.

4

I interesting	4 interesting
2 interested	5 interested
3 interesting	

Extend the activity to include the opposite of *interested / interesting – bored / boring*. Ask students to tell you when they are bored, what they find boring.

With a strong class, ask if they know any other words like this. Possible answers: *surprised, excited, amused, fascinated, terrified, frightened.*

5 Give students time to study the list and pick the adjectives which apply to their products or services and then add more of their own. Ask students to write their sentences as in the examples.

PX Ask students to think of two well-known products or services in the local market – preferably two competitors. If possible, show them advertising leaflets from the products and services. Why are the product services special?

Explaining what you need

I Individual then groupwork checking. Ask students to mark the stress, then practise pronouncing all the words from the box, then label the photographs.

I a carousel	5 a lectern
2 a remote control	6 a marker
3 a microphone	7 a socket
4 a projector	8 a flip chart

2 As Student's Book.

The structure *a thing to do something* involves the infinitive of purpose. Ensure that students are using this structure, and not using *for* or *for to do*.

a projector, a flip-chart, a remote control, a microphone, a carousel, a lectern, a marker, a socket

3 As Student's Book.

Size and dimension

KEY LANGUAGE POINT: Students at this level will probably know the adjectives *long, wide, high,* and *heavy*. Therefore the main point here is linking each to its associated noun and showing other ways of talking about weight.

I As Student's Book. Practise pronunciation of all the words and sentences, especially the difficult consonant clusters at the end of *length* and *width*. Point out similarity of spelling but difference of pronunciation in *height* and *weigh(t)*.

2 With a weak class, build up this conversation on the board in preparation for Activity 3.

Otherwise as Student's Book. It is probably best if students use phones and sit back to back. With small groups, your could use the internal phone system if feasible.

3 As Student's Book. Pairwork. One person looks at the information on page 43 of the Student's Book and the other person looks at the File on page 158.

They will need two trailers which will cost £3,500.

Pronunciation ⌊12⌋

The phonemic script is gradually introduced during the course. Show how the symbol relates to the diphthong in this case. Play the cassette and do one or two as examples. Tell students not to worry if they can only think of one spelling as they hear the word. Give them time to look at the words again after listening to think of a second spelling.

1	write / right	6	two / to / too
2	meet / meat	7	four / for
3	wood / would	8	there / their / they're
4	know / no	9	bye / buy / by
5	here / hear		

Sorting words

1   This is designed to assist learners in organizing, and taking charge of, their own learning.

2   As Student's Book. Possible answers:

truck	– a drawing, because it's concrete
inefficient	≠ efficient
component	– translation, because it's difficult to explain
weight	– explanation
reliable	– example sentence, because of collocation

3   After students have constructed the table, check pronunciation especially changing vowels – *sell* and *sale* and shifting stress – 'advertise and ad'vertisement.

verb	noun	noun (people)
to pro'duce	pro'duction	pro'ducer
to sell	sale	'salesperson
to 'advertise	ad'vertisement	'advertiser
to 'manage	'management	'manager
to em'ploy	em'ployment	em'ployer / emplo'yee

4   This is the first activity on collocation – the way words often go with other words. It is a very important aspect of English vocabulary, for example, we say *to make a mistake* but *to do something wrong*. There is often no logic to collocation; the students must simply learn it. Possible answers:

to make	money friends a profit a loss an enquiry a telephone
to update to deliver to package to buy to advertise to improve	a product

5   This is the first activity on lexical sets – another important aspect of vocabulary. Word networks may assist some students in learning and recalling vocabulary.

Construction materials	plastic, steel, rubber, paper
Market sector	domestic, commercial
Dimensions	length, width, etc.
Shape	circular, square, etc.
Design	sophisticated, advanced
Selling points	easy maintenance

24

SKILLS WORK

Optional equipment and materials

Some direct mail catalogues for Speaking 2

Speaking 1

As Student's Book. Get students to work in pairs and refer them to the crosswords on pages 46 and 159.

Listening

1 Use general questions and illustration as a warm-up.

2 As Student's Book.

Padded handlebar grips
Pull push handle bars
Adjustable seat
Liquid crystal speed and distance meter
Safety footstraps

---

3 ⬜13 Remind students what they are going to hear. Focus attention on the specifications box. Play the cassette once. Individual work, then pairwork checking. If they struggle, play the cassette again.

Length: 65 cm
Width: 38 cm
Height: 75–102 cm
Weight: 11 kilos

---

4 ⬜13 As Student's Book. Make sure students realize the manager is talking about two different models during his talk. Try to avoid defining or explaining words at this point – this is dealt with in Activity 5 below.

---
1 last year
2 sports centres
3 the domestic sector of the market
4 the domestic user
5 every member of the family
6 collapsible

---

5 You should not need to play the cassette again. Exploit as with all two-column matching activities.

---
1 c   2 f   3 g   4 a   5 d   6 e   7 b

Speaking 2

As Student's Book. Ask students to form groups of three or four.

If you have access to direct mail catalogues – particularly the kind with innovative experimental products in them – select some unusual items to continue the activity.

PRESENTATION

A lot of the vocabulary will be new, especially for pre-experience students. It is, however, very hard to pre-teach any of the vocabulary without a context. Therefore explain to students that they will understand the new words as the lesson continues.

1 [14] Ask students to read the list of stages. Ask them to guess the order of the stages before you play the cassette. Encourage discussion if students disagree. Do not confirm or correct yet.

Play the cassette once for students to get a general idea. Play again for them to number the stages. Pause between stages for thinking and writing.

Pairwork comparison, then conduct feedback, getting the correct order onto the board. Tell students not to worry if there are still words they don't understand.

1	run a feasibility study
2	design and construct the prototype
3	run tests
4	prepare detailed drawings
5	send drawings to the customers
6	modify designs
7	shelve project

2 [14] As Student's Book. Put the table on the board and complete it with student feedback.

1	Feasibility study	1991
2	Prototype design	1992
3	Tests	Autumn 1992 - June 1993
4	Preparation of detailed drawings and specifications	June - December 1993
5	Design modification	End 1993 - end 1994

3 As Student's Book. Play the cassette once more if necessary. Continue adding feedback to the table.

1	technical problems
2	Lots of things customers didn't like
3	short-staffed, computer problems
4	similar products on the market so they couldn't make a profit on line

Check vocabulary at this stage through reverse dictionary or sentence completion.

Pronunciation

KEY LANGUAGE POINT: The most important thing here is not that students **produce** perfect regular Past Simple endings, but that they realize some regular past tense endings have the extra syllable /ɪd/. Work on production too, but spend more time on recognition.

1 [15a] Check that students are aware of the three alternative pronunciations. Then play the cassette and get the students to follow the text in their Student's Book to develop their recognition of the different pronunciations.

2 [15b] As Student's Book. Students should work individually and then follow with pairwork checking.

/d/	/t/	/ɪd/
prepared	discussed	started
showed	looked	provided
discovered	liked	corrected
changed	asked	included
complained	finished	wanted

LANGUAGE WORK

Company history

KEY LANGUAGE POINT: There are two types of *wh-* question.

In the first type we don't know the subject, for example, *Something happened – What happened?*

In the second type we don't know the object, for example, *The company did something in 1925 – What did the company do in 1925?*

The key point is that only with subject questions can we use the Past Simple verb. With object questions we must use the auxiliary *did* and the infinitive (without *to*) of the main verb (the stem).

1 Work through the Nissan text with the whole class asking *What happened in ...?* (Using the dates).

Check the vocabulary. Put students in pairs for controlled practice.

All the verbs in the left-hand column of the article are regular, while all those in the right-hand column are irregular.

2 Work through the text with the whole class asking *When did ...?* The students can cover the text and use the pictures as prompts.

3 As Student's Book. Individual written activity, then pairwork checking.

1	imported	11	supplied
2	sold	12	achieved
3	had	13	was able to
4	grew	14	set up
5	was	15	started
6	became	16	were
7	decided	17	launched
8	found	18	won
9	began	19	was
10	had to		

4 This activity provides slightly freer practice of the two types of Past Simple question. Pairwork.

Saying *when*

KEY LANGUAGE POINT: There are no real rules for using time prepositions but there are some guidelines. We use *at*, *in*, and *on* with some regularity as follows:

1 Procedure as for other activities with table and exercises. Here is a further table which may help students:

in	on	at
years, centuries	days of the week	hours of the clock
months	dates	religious festivals
seasons	named days (Christmas Day)	points in time
parts of the day (with the)		parts of the day (noon/midday)

Cover the lists and try to remember the items.

Notice that some common time references do not require a preposition: *yesterday, last night, last year.*

1	on	6	at
2	in	7	at
3	on	8	in
4	in	9	at
5	in		

2 As Student's Book.

1	in	7	at
2	on	8	on
3	on	9	in
4	in	10	in
5	at	11	at
6	in	12	at

3 Change prompts 1, 2, 6 and 8 if necessary, depending on your students.

Reporting on a trip

1 As Student's Book.

> **1** Where did you go?
> **2** How did you travel?
> **3** How long did the journey take?
> **4** Where did you stay?
> **5** How long did you stay?
> **6** Why did you go?
> **7** Was the trip successful?

2 As Student's Book except for pre-experience students. Pairwork.

PX Change 'business trip' to 'holiday', unless students prefer to invent answers.

Complaints

1 [16a] Students can close books and listen, or listen and read at the same time. Only Flora's voice appears on the recording. Play cassette once and ask what students think the complaint is about – play again if necessary. Check that students understand that it is a complaint about a wrong delivery – the wrong delivery of a certain quantity of goods. Next ask them to suggest precisely what Roger said. Then put students in pairs to write in the missing words of the dialogue. Do not correct at this stage.

2 [16b] Allow them to correct their ideas for Roger's side of the dialogue – from Exercise 1 – from the recording. Then refer them to File 20 at the back of their books. Allow pairs to act out the telephone call. They should be able to recall most of the conversation without referring to their books.

3 Build up the conversations gradually putting them on the board first. Draw attention to the use of the pronouns, then demonstrate the activity with a good student. Put students in pairs to continue.

This is controlled practice so check that students are using the correct regular Past Simple endings and correct question structures.

4 As Student's Book. Encourage students to make up excuses for the problems in Number 3.

5 Putting the phrases in the correct place in the table is a good comprehension check. Adding further phrases is even better. Point out similarities of structure in the phrases in each group.

> *Dealing with complaints*
>
> **Making offers**
> c Would you like a refund?
> e Would you like us to repair it?
>
> **Promising action**
> a I'll find out what happened and let you know.
> d I'll look into it straight away.
>
> **Refusing responsibility**
> b I'm afraid we're not responsible for damage in transit.
> f We're very sorry about this but it's not worth it.

6 This is a much freer practice activity than 3. Demonstrate with a good student before putting into pairs.

7 As Student's Book. Pairwork.

SKILLS WORK

Reading

1 and **2** Read the first case with the whole class, elicit suggestions for what went wrong. Students work in groups on other cases and discuss why the products didn't sell. See if students can come up with their own suggestions before they do the exercise.

Ask students if they know of any other cases like this.

> 9 4 2 5 10 6 8 1 7 3

3 This is a scanning activity – searching a text for specific information. Individual activity with perhaps a time limit and a winner.

> **1** advert, ad
> **2** advertisers
> **3** commercial

Speaking

Allow time to prepare for this talk but agree a time limit. Instruct students to write notes – key words not full sentences. If some students have been involved in the same project, they can work together and make a joint presentation.

In small classes, students can take turns to give their presentations to the whole class, but divide large classes into groups. Before the speakers begin, remind the other students to listen carefully and ask questions to get more information. If they don't understand, they should ask the speaker to clarify.

PX Ask students to consider something which they have been involved in as part of a club or society. If some students cannot think of anything, put them with people who have an idea and let them construct a joint presentation.

6 Socializing

PRESENTATION

> **Optional equipment and materials**
> OHT of gapped conversation for Activity 2

1 `17a`

1 Write the word *socializing* on the board and ask students to tell you what it involves. Teach / elicit some of the vocabulary from this unit, including: *entertaining, visitor, conversation, meals, food, drink.*

Point out how important it is to be able to socialize with business contacts in order to form good business relationships.

Make sure students understand that they are going to hear several conversations between the same two people.

Ask students to read the T/F sentences.

Play the cassette once. Individual then pairwork checking.

If there is disagreement, play the cassette again.

a	false	Kevin says, 'It's great to see you again.'
b	true	
c	false	it took 1 hour
d	false	he wants it black

2 As Student's Book.

2 `17b`

1 As Student's Book.

a	true	
b	false	tomorrow
c	false	
d	true	

2 Ask students to try to remember this part of the conversation. Then show them – with OHT of 2.2 from the Student's Book if possible – how you can substitute other ideas into this gapped conversation. Then put them in pairs to practise talking about their own area and interests. Answers will differ.

3 `17c` As Student's Book. Deal with acceptable alternatives after students have listened to the cassette. Possible answers:

1	kind / sort
2	prefer / like
3	Sweet
4	often
5	have / try
6	like

LANGUAGE WORK

> **Optional equipment and materials**
> Lexical set activity for Interests and Routines 1
> Word square for Interests and Routines 2
> Cards with comments and questions from Chatting 3

Business lunches

1 As a warm-up, brainstorm food vocabulary, especially food that students like. If students are getting stuck on one type of food, ask for more starters or main courses, or puddings.

Teach or elicit the categories that the students will need for Activity 2 although you do not need to make absolutely sure that students can discriminate between them accurately at this stage.

Match the dishes.

> 1 Garden soup
> 2 Dover Sole
> 3 Chocolate Fudge Cake
> 4 Strawberries and cream
> 5 Leg of lamb
> 6 Duck
> 7 Summer Pudding
> 8 Cheese Tart
> 9 English cheeses
> 10 Smoked Salmon

2 With a strong class, do this as a quiz with a time limit and winners.

Adding extra words is a final check of understanding. Encourage students to use bi-lingual dictionaries if they wish.

meat	fish	poultry	vegetables	fruit
pork	salmon	chicken	peas	strawberries
beef	sole	duck	cauliflower	raspberries
lamb				cherries

There is often a different word in English for the animal and its meat.

Check that students know the animals which each meat comes from especially *ham*, *bacon*, *pork* and *gammon* from *pig*.

You could ask students to make their favourite foods into a menu.

3 Group work. As Student's Book. Give plenty of time for this activity. You might like to play the part of a rather surly waiter or waitress who misunderstands orders and asks for them to be repeated, then brings the wrong food.

Offers

KEY LANGUAGE POINT: Revision of countables and uncountables. Also how to make uncountables countable by putting them into containers or stating quantities.

Make sure students know that we use *a / an* with countable nouns. We can use *some* with countable and uncountable nouns.

1 Get students to look at the examples of the use of *a* + single uncountable, *some* + uncountable, and *some* + plural countable.

Teach / elicit the food and drink items in the illustration.

2 As Student's Book. Help students to build up countables like *a piece of cake*.

Teach, elicit the phrases *a ... of* and build up a table on the board or OHP with the students. Students can then make up sentences.

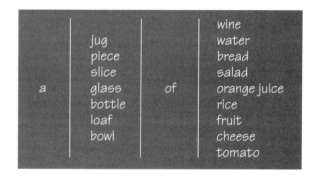

Pronunciation ⌗18

This conversation practices /tʃ/, /s/ and /ʃ/ sounds. Make sure students can pronounce the sounds in isolation before you begin. Play the cassette and let the students listen once or twice. Then stop after each sentence from the customer and get students to repeat. You could treat the waiter's part as a game (it is spoken on the cassette as a tongue-twister) and see how fast students can say it. Then pairwork.

Interests and routines

1 Point out that in social situations with business contacts we often talk about interests. We can ask about interests with *sort / kind / type*. Refer students to the table and the word boxes.

Check usage of the vocabulary from the word boxes with a lexical set activity as follows.

biographies classical comedies folk jazz musicals novels pop romances science fiction thrillers westerns detective stories rock horror		
books	films	music

4 Remind students of the frequency adverbs and teach or elicit the correct order, then check with the graphic.

Pairwork questioning then conduct feedback on what the other person does, for example, *S/he often reads La Stampa.*

Chatting

1 Social quiz. This is probably best done as pairwork, competitively.

1	b and c	6	c
2	a and c	7	a and c
3	a and c	8	b
4	b	9	c
5	b	10	a and c

2 1 Another area of interest for many people is sport. How many sports can the students name from the pictures?

Collocation activity. There is some logic here: sports which involve a ball and/or teams are normally *played*, whereas we use *go* for individual activities. Some modern activities, for example, karate, collocate with *do*.

play	go	do
tennis	swimming	judo/karate
golf	sailing	yoga
football/soccer	jogging/running	keep fit/aerobics

2 Here are some possible answers:

play	go	do
rugby	rowing	martial arts
basketball	walking	weightlifting
squash	bowling	
chess	hiking	
baseball	camping	
badminton	windsurfing	

3 As Student's Book.

3 Check the meaning of *routine*. Pairwork

For working students, as Student's Book.

PX Students can think of somebody they know – a parent perhaps and answer the question *How often does he/she …?*

2 Pairwork. Encourage students to try to find 5 unusual things they have in common. Perhaps work with a student to demonstrate one or two examples before starting the activity.

3 This could be done as in the Student's Book or with the comments printed on cards, which are passed from student to student, once a reply has been elicited.

4 As Student's Book.

1	h	5	l	9	a
2	k	6	g	10	e
3	d	7	i	11	f
4	j	8	b	12	c

SKILLS WORK

Speaking

Get students to change partners periodically.

Reading

1 This is a prediction activity to prepare the students for the reading text on page 67 of the Student's Book. It is best if students note down their answers before starting to read.

Students will also be interested to find information about their own country, if included, but this is focused on in Activity 4 below.

2 As Student's Book.

> **1** He washes up and sits down in front of the TV with a Scotch.
> **2** Professional people with a high income, educational level or occupational status.
> **3** They generally buy cars made in their own country.

3 Ask students to write five questions about the things they found most interesting in the chart. Then continue with pairwork questioning.

4 Decide beforehand whether to do this as a discussion of accuracy or whether you will ask students to suggest the statistics for their own country.

5 Put students into groups to compose the questions, then conduct the survey. Turn the results into a table.

PRESENTATION

1 🔲 Ask students what people do at meetings. Teach or elicit some of the following vocabulary: *present information*, *make proposals*, *discuss problems*, *make decisions*, *consider alternatives*.

Go through the instructions – check what a sales rep does.

Play the cassette once for students to get used to the voices. Ask them who speaks first – Nancy – who speaks next – Marcel – and who speaks last – Carlos.

Play the cassette again for students to complete the task.

Don't worry about the exact language at this stage – this is the focus of Activity 3 below.

Alternatives	Marcel	Carlos	Nancy
recruit new Spanish sales reps	A	F	F
transfer French sales reps	F	A	A

With good students: ask who they think the chairperson is (Nancy) and what they think the decision is going to be – recruit new Spanish sales reps probably, because the chairperson is in favour.

2 🔲 Remind students that after a meeting minutes will usually be written. Give students time to read the gapped text and suggest ways to complete the sentences. Play the cassette again, pausing to give students time to write.

> 1 train them
> 2 transfer them
> 3 the product knowledge
> 4 years to learn a language
> 5 train a new sales rep
> 6 branch
> 7 nationals

3 🔲 Refer students to the list of phrases and the flowchart of the discussion. Give students plenty of time to suggest matches, and even to try to conduct the conversation using the phrases they have assigned.

Then play the cassette again for checking.

> 1 f   2 j   3 c   4 h   5 d   6 i
> 7 a   8 b   9 k   10 g   11 e

LANGUAGE WORK

KEY LANGUAGE POINT: The use of *should* to give advice. Remind students that after *should* we use the base form of the verb.

Recommending action

1 Put these two sentences on the board.

A *We need Spanish-speaking sales staff.*

B *I think we should teach the French sales staff Spanish.*

Point out that:

Speaker A is explaining a problem situation.

Speaker B is recommending action.

Draw students' attention to the word *should* in the second sentence.

Add C's sentence below to the dialogue on the board.

C *I think we shouldn't do that.*

Point out that we don't normally put the negative marker on *should* in this structure. Instead, we move it to the introductory verb. Change on the board as follows:

C *I don't think we should do that.*

Put students into pairs. One person is the chairperson. S/he states the problem. The other person recommends a course of action:

A *We have a machine which is old and often breaks down.*

B *I think we should replace it* or *I don't think we should keep the machine.*

Monitor and provide feedback to the whole class on some of the best suggestions.

> 1 replace it
> 2 increase promotion budget
> 3 (not) use him any more
> 4 build a new one
> 5 (not) cut by so much
> 6 send him a warning letter

Encourage students to think of other answers. The more alternatives the better.

PX Ask students to decide which is the best alternative in each case.

2 Work through the first problem with a good student as an example. Then set as pairwork.

This is controlled practice so focus in on the language. Stop the activity and refocus if students are not using the appropriate forms.

Discuss as a whole class the best solution in each case. With better classes, ask them to give you suggestions as to any drawbacks with the solutions, for example, *Employ a teacher = expensive; send the staff to a language school = quality control.*

Asking for opinions

1 Check some of the vocabulary. As a change of pace this could be done as a whole class activity, especially with smaller classes.

2 As Student's Book.

3 Check vocabulary, then as Student's Book.

Making suggestions

Give students a few moments to study the language table. Then use the first situation to elicit suggestions from the class: *Why don't we run in-house English classes? Shall we employ an English teacher? We could send the staff to (name of good language school).*

At first, accept the ideas then start to reject them using sentences from the table.

Set the rest of the activity for pairs or small groups. Monitor and provide feedback with the best suggestions.

Justifying decisions

1 Remind students of the use of *be going to* for future plans or predictions about the future based on the present situation (for example, 2).

With a weaker class, go through the verb collocations before setting the activity.

Individual written practice.

> 1 They are going to stay in a hotel overnight.
> 2 He isn't going to arrive on time.
> 3 I'm not going to drink alcohol.
> 4 She's is going to send her assistant instead.
> 5 You aren't going to get good results this year.
> 6 We're going to park somewhere else.

2 This is a freer conversation practice activity.

Either do it as an individual activity, moving on to justifying the decisions in pairwork, or put students into small groups to conduct meetings about the meetings! Encourage the groups to think of a third alternative in each case before deciding what they are going to do. They must then justify their decisions to you, the boss.

Pronunciation

This is a minimal pairs exercise on some commonly confused words. The sentences are printed correctly in the Student's Book.

1 [20] Play the cassette once. Pause the cassette to allow students to decide how the sentence finishes, then play the complete sentence.

Practise the minimal pairs in isolation. Demonstrate the key difference in sound in each case.

1	work	4	lock
2	sit	5	leave
3	have		

2 As Student's Book.

Problem solving

1–3 This activity is in three parts and will take quite a lot of class time, but it is useful both as practice of the target language and to provide you with insights into your students' perceived learning difficulties. Allow plenty of time for it.

Answers to 3
1	c	4	a
2	b	5	d
3	e		

SKILLS WORK

Listening and writing

1 [21a] Ask students to look closely at the forms and predict what sort of language they are going to hear in the meeting.

Play the cassette section once to see how much they can get at first hearing. Monitor. Do not confirm or correct yet.

Play the cassette section again for checking and completion of the form. Pairwork checking.

Proposal	print special catalogue for multimedia products
Action plan	work out costs
Person responsible	Thierry
Review date	next Monday

2 [21b] Proceed as in Activity 1 above.

Proposal	keep sales office telephone lines open until 10pm
Action plan	take on more sales staff
Person responsible	Ulrike
Review date	3 months time

3 [21] Focus attention on the language. Ask the students to guess or remember as many of the words as they can, then play the cassette again for completion of the words and phrases.

1	work out
2	deal with
3	fill us in
4	get through
5	take on
6	take care of

As an extra activity you could give the verb and students then supply the preposition or particle, for example, *work – out*.

Speaking

1 Students read the proposals individually and choose savings totalling at least £1m. No group discussion should take place at this stage.

2 Assign the students to small groups to hold the meeting. Instruct them to make sure that everybody in the group contributes his/her view. Each group should appoint a secretary to take down details of the decisions – in the format used for Listening and writing above: *Proposal, Action Plan, Person responsible, Review date.*

8 Making Arrangements

PRESENTATION

> **Optional equipment and materials**
>
> OHT of diary page for Activity 1
>
> Phones for optional role-play after Activity 2
>
> Handout with jumbled conversation for Activity 3

1 22 Use the diary illustration to set the scene for this unit. Ask students if they keep a diary, what they write in it. Explain that you are going to talk about arrangements for the future.

Play the cassette once straight through (22a, 22b, and 22c), for students to get used to the voices. Check the instructions. Show what the students must do on the board or on an OHT of the diary page.

Play the cassette again, pausing at the end of each phone call. Provide feedback, working through the entries and the changes.

At the end of the three phone calls the diary entries should look like this:

> **Mon**   3 p.m. Mrs. Garcia Spanish Embassy
> **Tue**   11 a.m. Mrs Lonsdale
> **Wed**   2 p.m. Rindle UK Shareholders' Meeting
> **Thurs** 10 a.m. Golf with Patrick
>   10.30 a.m. Cristina García
> **Fri**   14.15 BA 297 Chicago

2 22 Focus the students' attention on the language in the conversations. Say that this time you want them to write the actual words spoken, where possible, not notes.

Play the cassette as necessary for the majority of students to get most of the sentences. Pairwork comparison and correction.

> **a** 1 Do you feel like playing golf some time next week?
>   2 See you on Thursday at ten, then.
> **b** 1 Would you like to come and see them one morning next week?
>   2 Because he's flying to Chicago.
>   3 I'll look forward to seeing you on Tuesday at eleven, then.
> **c** 1 I'm sorry, but I can't make it.
>   2 He's busy. He says 'I'm afraid I'm tied up then.'

Role-play the telephone call to Patrick to cancel the golf.

3 As Student's Book

> After this conversation he called Patrick to cancel the golf.

Pronunciation

1 23a This is mainly an ear training exercise. Students need to be able to distinguish good English intonation before they can begin to approximate to it. Pitch movement of any sort is the key point in polite intonation. Flatness sounds bored or rude.

Remind students what intonation is – the pattern of pitch movements through a phrase or sentence – by writing the first sentence on the board and drawing arrows to show the pitch movement as you speak.

Play several of the sentences to make sure that students know what to do. Then start from the beginning again and do the exercise.

> 1 good / flat   4 flat / good
> 2 flat / good   5 flat / good
> 3 good / flat

2 23b As Student's Book. Pairwork

Dates

1 ☐24 Set the problem. Do not confirm or correct yet.

Play the cassette and ask the question again.

Get the full spoken versions on the board, with the extra words for BrE. Then cross out *the* and *of* for the written version.

> In BrE 6/10 is the 6th of October, but in AmE it is the 10th of June.

2 Pairwork. As Student's Book.

LANGUAGE WORK

> **Optional equipment and materials**
> Handout for Timetables 2
> Phones for Fixing a time 3

KEY LANGUAGE POINT: In these exercises, two forms of the present tense are used to talk about the future – Present Simple for timetabled future, Present Continuous for arranged future. The difference is small, but learnable. We use the Present Simple to talk about the future which has been written down in a timetable. We use the Present Continuous to talk about the future which has been arranged with others.

Timetables, plans, and arrangements

1 As Student's Book.

With a weak class, dictate a series of times for students to write as numbers, for example, *Half past nine – 9.30.*

There is a difference between BrE and AmE in telling the time.

	BrE	AmE
3.45	a quarter to four	a quarter of four
4.15	a quarter past four	a quarter after four
4.30	half (past) four	half (past) four

2 As Student's Book with a good class.

With a weak class, give a series of questions, on the board or on a handout as below. Set a time limit to find the answers.

> *Alternative activity*
>
> 1 When does the conference take place?
>   ....
>
> 2 Where do the participants have lunch?
>   ....
>
> 3 What time do they hear the Regional Report from Spain? ....
>
> 4 How often do the shuttlebuses go to the airport? ....
>
> 5 What time does the *Mange Tout* restaurant close for dinner? ....
>
> 6 How much do the coach tours cost for adults?
>   ....
>
> 7 What time does *Highlights* open?
>   ....
>
> 8 How long does the Roof Top Barbecue last?
>   ....

Then get students to cover the questions and try to write them in their notebooks, from the answers and the information in the conference programme.

> 1 on July 22nd
> 2 at Swithins Restaurant
> 3 at 2.30 p.m.
> 4 every three hours from 7.00 to 19.00
> 5 at 11.00 p.m.
> 6 £8.00
> 7 at 9.45 a.m.
> 8 for 4 hours

3 Go through the itinerary asking questions around the class before moving on to pairwork.

> **Possible questions to ask**
>
> What's he doing at 10.15 / at 11.45?
> When / Where is he having lunch?
> When is he going on a tour of the factory?
> What's he doing after lunch?
> When is he leaving for Heathrow?
> When does his flight leave for Germany?

Draw attention to the Present Continuous tense and contrast situation with Activity 1 above – timetable vs. arrangements.

Making appointments

1 [25] Pairwork then check by playing the cassette. Draw attention to the fixed phrase *I'll look forward to seeing you*. In this case, *then* is used to confirm the arrangement.

> 6 2 9 4 10 3 8 5 7

2 As Student's Book.

> 1 fix
> 2 How about
> 3 tied up
> 4 be convenient
> 5 manage
> 6 make it

3 Written individual work. Deal with any extra vocabulary before starting the activity.

> 1 have
> 2 be late for
> 3 make
> 4 cancel
> 5 postpone

If you *cancel* a meeting you stop it altogether but if you *postpone* it you arrange it for a later date.

4 This is probably best done as a high speed oral activity. Students think up their own sentences using cancel and postpone and then look at File 10 and then File 21 for the answers.

Cancel	a flight, a holiday, an order, a visit, a dinner, a meeting, an appointment, a booking
Postpone	a visit, a meeting, a holiday, a dinner

Invitations

KEY LANGUAGE POINT: We vary our language according to the formality of the situation. Make sure, throughout this section, that students recognize the difference between the formal situations and the informal ones.

1 Formal phrases. Practise the phrases with the whole class before going on to pairwork. Check the intonation.

2 and **3** Informal phrases. Procedure as above.

Fixing a time

1 There are a lot of tables of phrases in this unit. If you are doing the whole Language Work section in one lesson, you might like to vary the presentation here – perhaps put the tables on the board with gaps for the students to fill in and copy down, then check with the Student's Book.

Allow plenty of time for working through the 'map' of the conversation before starting the pairwork.

2 Group work as in Student's Book.

3 Pairwork. Back to back, with phones if available.

> **Possible answer**
> Friday 9–11 a.m. or Saturday in the day time

SKILLS WORK

Writing

1 As Student's Book.

> It is about Mr Nakagawa's inspection visit (Re = *about, concerning*)
> Points of difference with letters may include: information such as *Attention, Re:* often given in a box at the top; often no salutation (*Dear Sir,* etc.); the number of pages is specified – in case some are missed or garbled; complimentary close is often *Regards / Best wishes* rather than *Yours.*

2 As Student's Book. Students work in two groups using different information from page 86 of the Student's Book and File 11 on page 159. See possible answers opposite, page 41.

Speaking

1 Allow around 30 minutes to complete. Use the phones again and sit back to back if feasible.

Once each pair has finished let them check their answers to make sure they have both written down the same schedule.

> **Possible answers**
>
> | | | |
> |---|---|---|
> | **Mon** | 9–12 | Mrs Carne |
> | | 12–2 | Lunch with Dave Czernovicz |
> | | 2–5 | Miss Carley |
> | **Tues** | 9–11 or 10–12 | Mr Gandhi |
> | | 12–2 | Reception |
> | **Wed** | 9–11 or 10–12 | Ms Lyon |
> | | 1–5 | Factory tour, Mr Barnes |

2 This exercise is much more difficult but reassure students that it can be done:

> | | | |
> |---|---|---|
> | **Mon** | 9–12 | Mrs Carne |
> | | 12–2 | Lunch with Dave Czernovicz |
> | | 2–5 | Miss Carley |
> | **Tues** | 9–1 | Mrs Barnes |
> | | 1–3 | Ms Lyon |
> | | 3–5 | Mr Gandhi |

Janet's first reply to Masahiro.

To: Nihon Informalink KK	Attention: Masahiro Nakagawa
From: Janet Jeffries	Re: Your visit to the UK
Date: 11 June 1996	Pages: 1

Thank you for your fax of 10 June. I will meet you at Heathrow at 16.35 on 16 June. As you requested, I have booked you a single room at the Dorchester for 2 nights. If your wife is travelling with you I will have to change the booking.

I have also arranged a meeting for you with Data Link on 17 June.

I'll see you next week.

Best regards,

Janet Jeffries

Masahiro's first fax to Janet regarding his change of plans.

To: Darworth Enterprises	Attention: Janet Jeffries
From: Masahiro Nakagawa	Re: Revised travel plans, UK
Date: 11 June 1996	Pages: 1

I am very sorry but I have to change my flight arrangements for next week. I will now be arriving on 15 June, the day before my original flight. My new flight number is BA 018 and arrival time is 18.55 at Terminal 4, Heathrow.

Could you also rearrange my meeting with Data Link for 16 June - please let me know if this is difficult.

Thank you very much.

Best regards,

Masahiro Nakagawa

Masahiro's second fax to Janet which crossed with hers.

To: Darworth Enterprises	Attention: Janet Jeffries
From: Masahiro Nakagawa	Re: Revised travel plans, UK
Date: 12 June 1996	Pages: 1

Thank you for your fax dated 11 June. Thank you for organizing my flights and hotel booking - but I am afraid my plans have changed. I am now arriving a day early on 15 June.

You will by now have received a fax with details of my new dates and flight information. I am sorry for all the trouble you have gone to.

Best regards,

Masahiro Nakagawa

Janet's second reply to Masahiro.

To: Darworth Enterprises	Attention: Masahiro Nakagawa
From: Janet Jeffries	Re: Revised travel plans, UK
Date: 12 June 1996	Pages: 1

Thank you for your fax dated 11 June.

I have no problem changing your flight to the UK. You are now booked on Flight Number BA 018 to arrive at 18.55 on 15 June, Terminal 4, Heathrow airport. I will be there to meet you.

Changing your meeting with Data Link to 16 June was more difficult. The Director is not free on that day. Could you make it for the following day instead, 10am? Please let me know if this is not possible. Perhaps you could give me some idea of a convenient day for you?

I look forward to seeing you soon.

Best regards,

Janet Jeffries

41

9 Describing Trends

PRESENTATION

> **Optional equipment and materials**
> OHTs of graphs on pages 88 and 89

1 It is probably best to do this as a deep-end activity, with no lead in, just to find out what students know already.

Individual written, then pairwork checking. Give feedback, using OHT of the graphs to indicate correct (and incorrect).

Don't do detailed work on the vocabulary which this exercise raises – explain that you will deal with it during the unit.

Graph 2 – *decreased by* 2% not *to* 2%.

Graph 4 – *sharply* means there must be quite a large increase on the previous months.

Graph 5 – *slightly* means the increase must be small.

1
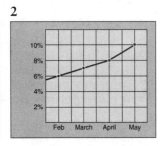

2

3
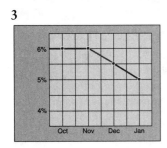

4
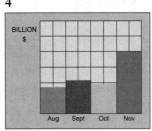

5
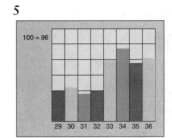

6
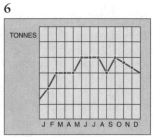

2 [26] You may need to play the cassette several times.

Individual written and pairwork checking. Give feedback as above.

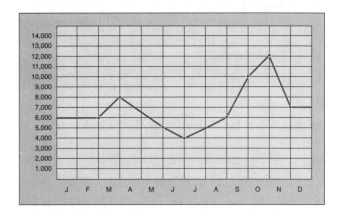

3 [26] Point out that graphs only show you **what** happened. They don't tell you why.

Set the activity and play the cassette again; be prepared to play twice if necessary.

If students are apparently struggling even after several hearings, refer them to the tapescript on page 187 to check their ideas.

Instead of asking students to write out the sentences of explanation, you could show them how to annotate the graph, with flags at the key points and the reason written on the flag – as in some magazines.

> 1 The Spring sales campaign began.
> 2 Their competitors launched a rival product.
> 3 They increased their discounts to the wholesalers.
> 4 They received the Christmas orders.
> 5 Christmas orders stopped.

Students ask and answer about the events and the reasons why they happened:

Why did sales increase in March?
Because the Spring sales campaign began.

4 Point out that prepositions are very important in discussion of movements.

Show the difference between *Sales went down by 1,000* and *Sales went down to 1,000.* We use *by* to describe the difference and *to* to talk about the point reached.

For this reason, it is worth spending some time on this and dealing with mistakes during feedback.

Set up activity for individual written work then pairwork checking.

Use an OHT if available to check answers during the feedback session.

1	at	**5**	from / to
2	from / to	**6**	by
3	by	**7**	at
4	to		

5 This is an extra activity on prepositions.

1	in (invest in)
2	on (spend on)
3	on (waste on)
4	from (make from)
5	on (save on)
6	to (give to)
7	from (borrow from)
8	to (owe to)

LANGUAGE WORK

Rises and falls

1 Point out that there is virtually no difference in meaning between the verbs in each set, although *go up / down* is more informal than the others.

Practise pronunciation of the verbs. Check that students know the past tenses.

Set up pairwork. Point out that the information in each line is linked either through cause and effect or through one offsetting the other, for example, *market share* and *turnover*; *distribution costs* and *prices of raw materials.*

Practise the pronunciation of most, if not all, of the words here.

2 As Student's Book.

PX Because the answers to the exercise above can be invented – indeed, will have to be by all but perhaps accountants or senior managers – there is no reason why pre-experience students shouldn't do this activity. Give them a scenario of a very successful company and ask them to imagine what went up and what went down last year. And then give them an unsuccessful company.

Answers depend on students.

Pronunciation

1 and **2** [27] As Student's Book.

1	write	**7**	sign
2	know	**8**	business
3	answer	**9**	half
4	receipt	**10**	scientist
5	listen	**11**	chemist
6	high	**12**	psychiatrist

43

Describing changes

1 **First table**. Point out that verbs can often be used as nouns with no change of form, but that sometimes the form changes. Ask students to complete the table, deciding in each case if a change in form is necessary. During feedback, check stress shift between verb and noun where applicable.

> 2 *a fall*
> 3 *an increase*: note shift in stress from verb *to increase*
> 4 *a decrease*: note shift in stress from verb *to decrease*
> 5 *an improvement*
> 6 *a recovery*

If the verb *to raise* is mentioned, show the difference with two sentences: *Last year prices rose by 3%. Many companies raised their prices.* There must be a real agent to use the verb *to raise* whereas we can say that 'things' rise.

Second table. The only difficulty here is the spelling of the adverb.

> sharply
> dramatically
> steadily

> 1 dramatic
> 2 sharp
> 3 slight
> 4 steady

2, 3, and **4** This set of activities could be done for homework. If done in class, vary the procedure for each set, for example, high-speed whole-class, individual, written, and pairwork discussion.

2	3	4
1 slight	1 dramatically	1 steadily
2 sharp	2 steadily	2 dramatic
3 dramatic	3 sharply	3 sharply
4 steady	4 slightly	4 slight
		5 sharp
		6 slightly
		7 dramatically
		8 steady

Steady/ily is normally used when a change has happened over several months or years.

Describing graphs

As Student's Book. At the end students compare the real graph and their own version and discuss reasons for differences. Pairwork.

Giving reasons

1 You will need to check the meaning of several vocabulary items before starting the activity but be careful not to pre-empt it through giving too many clues as to which account each fact would affect. Point out that students have to associate each event with a particular account, then see which month showed a significant change.

> 2 October
> 3 August
> 4 September
> 5 November
> 6 October

2 Work through the example on the board. Show how the reason and result can be given in either order but that this affects the linking verb. Pairwork.

44

3 As Student's Book. Individual written activity.

4 Individual work, then pairwork checking.

> **1** led to / resulted in
> **2** resulted from / were due to
> **3** led to / resulted in
> **4** resulted from / was due to
> **5** led to / resulted in
> **6** resulted from / were due to
> **7** led to / resulted in
> **8** resulted from / was due to

SKILLS WORK

> **Optional equipment and materials**
> Large sheets of paper / OHT blanks and pens for Speaking 2

Speaking

1 As Student's Book. Pairwork.

PX Suggest an area which you feel your students might be familiar with – for example, sales of a seasonal item.

2 As Student's Book.

If possible students should produce their final graphs in a form which can be displayed – large sheets of paper or OHTs.

Reading

1 This is to get students thinking about the subject. Do not confirm or correct yet.

2 This activity exploits the fact that the first sentence in most paragraphs in English is a 'topic' sentence – in other words it sets the thematic tone for the paragraph. Students should therefore be able to work out which topic sentence begins each paragraph. Topic sentences enable native speakers to skim a text quickly to find key information or to get the gist.

Explain this to your students to justify the activity.

Students should try to do the activity individually and then in pairs or groups.

Try to avoid giving the answers from the front.

When students have got the answers, you might ask them to explain how they worked them out.

> 4   7   1   6   3   2   5

3 Students can use a dictionary to check their guesses.

4 As Student's Book. Pairwork.

> **Possible questions to ask**
> **1** Who was Asa Candler?
> **2** When did the first bottling plant open?
> **3** Why did sales dramatically rise in 1892?
> **4** Where was Asa Candler from?
> **5** What did Asa Candler do to promote Coca-Cola?
> **6** How much was a glass of Coke in 1886?

PRESENTATION

1 The warm-up questions are for students in work.
PX Ask students the same questions about the institute or school you are teaching in.

2 Check the item *call-out* – a visit from an engineer to repair something which has broken down. Pairwork, then conduct a feedback session: students give you the answers and you reconstruct the table on the board. In order for you to be able to reconstruct the table, the students will have to give you the information in the form below. Keep questioning until they do give it in this form.

> **1** They received 803 call-outs in September.
> **2** They try to answer 80% of the call-outs within 4 hours.
> **3** They try to repair 90% of the machines within 24 hours.
> **4** Yes, they exceeded the first target by 4.6% and the second by 1.9%.

You can get the students to calculate for you that 80 + 4.6 = 84.6% of 803 = 679, and 90 + 1.9 = 91.9% of 803 = 738.

These words are practised later: *miss, achieve, exceed your target*.

3 [28] Get the blank table for the October figures on to the board, and ask students to give you the figures which are already entered. If students are poor at giving you figures, deliberately put in the wrong figures until they get it exactly right. Play the cassette once or twice to allow students to complete the table.

	October		
	Call-outs	Calls answered within 4 hours	Machines repaired within 24 hours
Number	**880**	**705**	732
Percentage		80%	83.2%
Target		80%	90%
Difference		0%	− 6.8%

4 Play the cassette again for students to get the reason.

> They have had trouble getting spare parts from the warehouse.

5 [28] As Student's Book.

> **A** How far, yet
> **B** I have
> **A** —
> **B** has gone
> **A** We've been
> **B** risen
> **A** achieved

LANGUAGE WORK

> **Optional equipment and materials**
> Copies of the vocabulary handout for Giving News; Phones for Checking progress 5

KEY LANGUAGE POINT: This section practises the Present Perfect of six common verbs of movement – the Past Simple forms were practised in Unit 9. Make sure your students know the past participles.

Giving news

1 Useful financial vocabulary items are involved here, so give students plenty of time to work out which is which.

A profit and loss account shows the income and expenditure of a company over a certain period of time, usually a year. Students involved in finance can compare this format with similar accounts in their own company. Style and layout can vary between countries and companies.

Ask students whether they think this company is doing well or badly, and whether it is in a better condition this year than last, or worse. (It's not doing badly, but there was no real growth last year, which can be dangerous for a company.)

1	dividend
2	distribution costs
3	retained profit
4	administrative costs
5	cost of sales

2 Note that the question is about 'this year' – the suggestion is it hasn't yet finished (or its effects are still being felt) so we use the Present Perfect not the Past Simple. Some students may have learnt that we use the Present Perfect only to talk about events which haven't finished. In fact, we also use it to talk about the recent past when the effects are still present. Students can continue with further, similar questions about the profit and loss account.

3 Ask students what they would expect to find in a Chairman's Review. Do not confirm or correct yet.

Individual written activity, then pairwork checking.

1	has been	10	has continued
2	have reached	11	have introduced
3	have shown	12	have given
4	have fallen	13	have established
5	has grown	14	has assisted
6	have performed	15	have entered
7	have invested	16	have begun
8	has involved	17	have signed
9	have run		

4 As Student's Book except for pre-experience students. Pairwork.

PX Students should write about six things they have done in their college life, or in hobbies or sports outside college.

Staff changes

1 This could be done as a high-speed whole-class activity. It is, however, an important activity in that it sets the scene for Activity 2. It helps to avoid confusion over the use of the passive which is not a target here.

E	C
C	C
E	C
C	C
E/C	E

2 Ask students to find information quickly in the tables, then set the activity for written work.

1	resigned
2	retired
3	taken early retirement
4	(been) transferred
5	sacked/fired
6	fired/sacked
7	dismissed
8	made ... staff redundant
9	taken on
10	recruited

3 As Student's Book.

4 As Student's Book except for pre-experience students.

PX Students could ask you about changes at the institute/school. You don't have to tell the truth!

47

Targets

1 As Student's Book.

> 1 The East and the South-West
> 2 The West and the Midlands
> 3 The North and the South-East

2 As Student's Book.

1 Role-play between the Sales Manager and the Managing Director.

Sales Manager: Emphasize the good results.
Managing Director: Point out the weaknesses.

Alternative activity. Students could also write a report on one of the regions in the chart on page 103 of the Student's Book. In pairs, each student must guess which region they are talking about, for example, *This region sold 4,100 units last year. This year their target was 5,800 units but they only sold 5,650, which means that they have missed their target by 2.6%.* Answer: The South-East.

3 As Student's Book.

Allow different pairs to compare and discuss their results. The students must decide what criteria to use, therefore there is no right answer here.

> **Possible Answers**
>
> **Catherine** achieved the greatest increase in sales – 2,400 – and exceeded one target very well whilst just missing the other.
>
> **Carole** sold the largest number of both drugs – 9,650 but failed to reach one of her targets.
>
> **Peter** sold a large number of units – 9,150 – and exceeded one target but missed the other.

Checking progress

1 As Student's Book. Pairwork.

PX Some of these questions will be appropriate. Students could invent alternatives to the others.

2 As Student's Book. Students should concentrate on the 'Action Taken' column at this stage.

> She has written to Paul Sykes.
>
> She has received a letter from Sunita Advani.
>
> She has phoned Jorge Castano.
>
> She has sent some sales literature to Erica Williams.
>
> She has recieved a call from Kate Cowe.
>
> She has visited Michela Messina.
>
> She has had a meeting with Chris Murphy.

3 Students should now be combining information from the 'Action Taken' and 'To do' columns. There is some practice of the Present Perfect here but the main point is just business communication. A variety of dialogues are possible here. Pairwork.

4 [29] Ensure that students understand that the listening activity relates to the table on page 105. Pause after each phone call.

> Michela Messina, Jorge Castano, Kate Cowe, Sunita Advani, Chris Murphy, Paul Sykes, Erica Williams.

5 Simulate the phone call in pairs using phones or back to back.

SKILLS WORK

> **Optional equipment and materials**
> Phones for Speaking Activity

Listening

1 🔲30 Set the scene and play the cassette once. Ask students how many items there are.

Play the cassette again and ask students what each item is about. Let students compare their notes.

> **Any variation on these notes:**
>
> **Item 1** Share price falls
> **Item 2** Drop in profits
> **Item 3** Poisoned tonic water
> **Item 4** Connecting human brains to computers

With higher level classes, ask students to note down any words they think are important from each item. Students compare words in groups.

2 🔲30 Give students plenty of time to read the target information required for each item. Stop after each item for students to write and then compare.

> 1 Share prices
> 2 Wall Street
> 3 leading computer companies
> 4 1987
> 5 50.2
> 6 British Gas
> 7 4%
> 8 warm winters, a fall in gas prices, rising competition
> 9 Safeway
> 10 Poison was discovered in 4 bottles on their shelves
> 11 The police aren't sure
> 12 The head of British Telecom's Martlesham Heath Laboratories
> 13 The human brain will be connected to computer chips
> 14 By the year 2000

Pronunciation

🔲31 Vowel sounds.

A key point here is the fact that vowel sounds cannot be predicted from spelling.

1	for	**4**	head
2	year	**5**	close
3	half	**6**	point

Speaking

Ask your students if they own any stocks and shares. Pre-teach *shares*, *stockbroker*, *portfolio* if necessary before beginning the activity.

Simulate the phone call in pairs using phones or back to back.

At the end students check next week's share prices on page 159 to see if they made the right decision.

PRESENTATION

1 Warm up through questions. Use the pictures to assist discussion.

PX Ask students to consider the building they study in, or, if that is not appropriate, to talk about a well-known public building in the area and about their homes.

2 [32] Allow students to study the plan and check vocabulary before listening. Be prepared to play the cassette several times if necessary. At this stage students need only identify the actual locations. Details will be studied in the following sections.

> **a** High security store
> **b** Gatehouse
> **c** Reception
> **d** Delivery and loading bay
> **e** Main store

3 Play again for students to complete the gap fill.

> **a** A: None
> Q: What will you keep
> Will there be
>
> **b** A: Check the traffic coming in and out
> Q: How many people
> How much equipment
>
> **c** A: Report to reception
> Q: won't be much ... will there?
> won't be many
>
> **d** A: It will be a busy area
> Q: will be
> will be
>
> **e** A: They open straight on to the car park
> Q: You'd better not
> You'd better

LANGUAGE WORK

Talking about quantity

1 Give students plenty of time to look at the brochure before asking warm-up questions – *Where is this? Would you like to go there?* etc.

Then ask the warm-up question in the Student's Book. Ask students to make a list of the reasons as they read, but don't give the answers as they form part of Activity 2.

2 Point out that we can describe the advantages of a place by saying what is and isn't there.

Remind students that the verb *to be* agrees with the object in these sentences: *There <u>are</u> a lot of ... <u>places to eat and drink</u>.*

Remind them also that *much* goes with uncountables, and *many* with countables: *There isn't <u>much</u> ... <u>traffic.</u>*

Also remind them that the sentences must say how good the place is for conferences.

Individual writing, then pairwork checking. Conduct feedback onto the board, correcting as necessary. After you have put up the correct sentence endings, rub off the openings and ask students to recall them.

> 1 conference equipment available / tropical vegetation
> 2 sports and leisure activities / different places to eat and drink
> 3 traffic / noise
> 4 places as beautiful as Phuket / cars
> 5 pressure / pollution
> 6 ringing telephones / difficult customers

3 Demonstrate the activity with one or two students. Put students in pairs for question and answer activity.

> **Possible questions:**
> 1 Is there much industry?
> 2 Is there much unemployment?
> 3 Are there many open spaces?
> 4 Are there many parks?
> 5 Are there many immigrants?
> 6 Are there many tourists?
> 7 Are there many old buildings?
> 8 Is there much traffic?
> 9 Are there many golf courses?
> 10 Are there many restaurants?
> 11 Is there much nightlife?
> 12 Is there much snow?

4 This could be done as a high-speed whole-class activity to change the pace. Alternatively, draw the table on the board for students to copy and work on individually or in pairs.

This activity leads into Activity 5.

> | | |
> |---|---|
> | information | U |
> | fact | C |
> | research | U |
> | money | U |
> | dollar ($) | C |
> | suggestion | C |
> | help | U |
> | advice | U |
> | job | C |
> | work | U |
> | man | C |
> | person | C |
> | machinery | U |
> | machine | C |
> | equipment | U |
> | furniture | U |
> | paper | U |
> | newspaper | U/C |
> | news | U |
> | time | U/C |
> | experience | U/C |

A few other countable words can also be uncountable (and vice versa) but the meanings are too obscure for this level.

Many uncountable nouns have a countable alternative: *We've collected some information / facts. Have you any advice / suggestions? He did some work / jobs.*

People is a countable noun. *People* is the common irregular plural of *person* in BrE.

Some nouns, such as *time*, can be both countable and uncountable, depending on context.

5 Individual written work.

> | | | | |
> |---|---|---|---|
> | 1 | much | 6 | many |
> | 2 | much | 7 | many |
> | 3 | many | 8 | much |
> | 4 | much | 9 | many |
> | 5 | many | 10 | much |

Making predictions

1 and **2** As Student's Book.

PX Ask students to make predictions about the economy of their country, the industry in the area, the standard of living. Students from the same country or area can work in groups.

Giving advice

Work through the example on the board. Demonstrate with a good student. Organize feedback by giving the situations again orally and getting advice from individual students. Check the form of the verb after *You'd better (not)*.

> **Possible answers**
> 1 You'd better query it / not pay it.
> 2 You'd better not sign it / You'd better read it again.
> 3 You'd better not employ him / her / find someone else.
> 4 You'd better not go / stay here.
> 5 You'd better find them quickly / postpone the presentation.
> 6 You'd better arrange another meeting, not negotiate the deal on your own.

Pronunciation

1 As Student's Book. Individual work, then pairwork checking.

1	are not	5	I have
2	will not	6	has not
3	you had	7	has
4	I would	8	she is

2 With a weak class, go through the sentences orally and then let the students do them again individually.

1	**He will** –	He'll	**he has** –	he's
2	**We have** –	We've	**I have not** –	I haven't (I've not)
3	**I am** –	I'm	**I would** –	I'd
4	**You had** –	You'd	**they have** –	they've
5	**does not** –	doesn't	**it is** –	it's

3 [33] Play the cassette for students to check.

Offering help

1 [34] As Student's Book. The students use the pictures to remind them what to say when they act out the conversation.

1	– (c)	4	– (b)
2	– (d)	5	– (a)
3	– (f)	6	– (e)

2 Pairwork. Act out the first suggestion with a good student first, and encourage students to be inventive.

Conference planning

1 Give students time to read advertisement on page 115 of the Student's Book and discuss in pairs.

2 The pictures are quite self-explanatory and students should be able to work out the conversation without your help, but you may need to provide some vocabulary.

Choose one or two pairs to perform their conversation in front of the class.

SKILLS WORK

Listening

1 [35a] Warm up by asking why companies move the location of their offices. Then set the scene. Give students time to read the stages of the move.

Play the cassette, several times if necessary.

move out	not known yet
lease	October
contract	next week
new building ready	by end of September
fix moving date	next month

2 [35a] Play the cassette again, focusing on key information.

He says they are tiny.

She explains that only half the staff will be there because of teleworking.

Teleworking is working, away from the office. Workers are linked to the office by telephone and/or computer link.

3 [35a] Play cassette again, focusing on form. After getting the answers on the board, ask students to rate them for how definite they sound.

plan to	definite
intend to	definite
expect to	indefinite
aim to	definite
hope to	speculative

4 General discussion leading to notes in a table of advantages and disadvantages. Ask if students know Ernst & Young, a company with many teleworkers. This exercise leads to Activity 5.

5 [35b] Ask students to check off any points they hear, or add any extra ones. Possible answers and board plan:

Advantages	Disadvantages
save on rent	staff need access to office equipment
reduce overheads (e.g. electricity)	staff won't like it
staff will enjoy working at home	difficult to check on work
no commuting	difficult to motivate
	not able to learn from colleagues

6 As Student's Book.

daily	quarterly	weekly	hourly	yearly/annual

The staff will come into the office for monthly meetings and they'll have daily contact with their supervisor by telephone.

Speaking

1 and **2** There are two parts: a planning (small groups) and a reporting back stage (whole class).

Some groups may be short of ideas to start with and you may need to make some suggestions: an office cleaning agency; a holiday tour company; a fast food restaurant; an executive language school.

Role-play the meeting with the bank manager (yourself or a very good student) to discuss the business plan.

53

PRESENTATION

1 Warm up through discussion of the visual. Put students into pairs to match the headings to the graphics. Students check their ideas with other students near them. If there is any disagreement, students explain their reasoning.

> A – pie chart, frozen foods.
> B – graph, desserts.
> C – table, ready meals.

2 [36] Explain that they are going to hear retailers talking about the three sets of figures. Set the task and play the cassette.

> **a** bar graph (B)
> **b** table (C)
> **c** pie chart (A)

3 [36a] As Student's Book.

> **1** False. They are about the same.
> **2** False
> **3** True
> **4** True

4 [36b] As Student's Book.

> **1** It's part of a general trend towards healthier diets
> **2** Pizzas

5 [36c] As Student's Book.

> **1** more mature, much wider, more adventurous
> **2** more competitive, lower

6 and **7** These two exercises call on the students to induct the rules for making comparative and superlative forms of adjectives. They could be done as class discussion. Help the students to come up with something close to the explanation below.

> We use -er and the -est with short adjectives. (all adjectives with one syllable and some adjectives with two syllables).
> We use more and the most with long adjectives (some adjectives with two syllables and all adjectives with three or more syllables).

There is more information on comparatives and superlatives on page 172 of the Student's Book.

LANGUAGE WORK

> **Optional equipment and materials**
> Adjective collocation handout for Comparing companies 4

Comparing sales figures

As a variation, ask students to complete this activity for homework before the lesson and then have a feedback session at the beginning of the next lesson.

3	wider	**12**	More casual
4	Cheaper	**13**	darker
5	more difficult	**14**	more popular
6	lower	**15**	more colourful
7	colder	**16**	slower
8	higher	**17**	better
9	Longer	**18**	worse
10	shorter	**19**	easier
11	more stylish		

Comparing countries

1 If feasible, give one graph each to six different groups. Get them to prepare the short paragraph and be ready to present the graph and the paragraph to the other students.

1	Russia	14	the least
2	Japan	15	More than
3	Thailand	16	less than
4	the highest	17	France
5	the lowest	18	Sweden
6	less	19	Switzerland
7	than	20	than
8	more	21	the fewest
9	than	22	the most
10	Tokyo	23	More
11	Singapore	24	than
12	Milan	25	more
13	the most	26	than

2 General discussion. Students should be encouraged to be anecdotal as well as statistically accurate!

Comparing companies

1 Do the first question as an example. Then set pairwork.

2 As Student's Book.

3 Group or even whole class discussion.

> This is a very difficult decision. None of the three companies is best or worst in all or most categories. The extra price you pay for Paper Packs is more than offset by the best terms of payment and the discount. The product range is good but delivery and quality record are not good. The Card Company comes out reasonably well, if you are not worried about the small product range.

Set students this task (optional), perhaps for homework: write a brief report to your Managing Director, recommending one of these companies and justifying your recommendation.

4 As Student's Book.

   PX Consider two large companies in a particular sector – locally or internationally. If necessary, get the students to research the topic and then discuss the questions in 4 above.

SKILLS WORK

Speaking 1

1 Show how to complete the chart by giving your personal ranking of 1, 2, and 3. Add one extra point of your own to demonstrate this feature of the activity. Pairwork.

2 As Student's Book. Check if students have any interesting differences. Pairwork

3 As Student's Book. Once again, check for any interesting differences.

Reading

1 The graphs are used to create anticipation.

   You could get students to actually write down what they think the article will be about. Do not confirm or correct yet.

2 Individual written work.

> They researched attitudes to travelling.
>
> They did it to show that teleconferencing (which does not require travelling) is better.

55

3 Individual written work then pairwork checking.

> meetings away
> checking in
> waiting for a flight to take off

4 and **5** Whole class activities.

> *Possible answers*
>
> | | |
> |---|---|
> | broker | dentist |
> | banker | psychiatrist |
> | teacher | typist |
> | lawyer | economist |
> | barrister | journalist |
> | reporter | artist |

6 As Student's Book. Link the reading text to the Speaking 2 activity which follows.

> Irritability and depression. Other symptoms could be exhaustion, a short temper, or ill health.

Speaking 2

1 Matching procedure as for all two-column activities. End with discussion of the final two questions.

> **1** g **2** c **3** b **4** h **5** e **6** a **7** d **8** f

2 Get students to mark their own ranking individually.

3 Students should compare in groups and perhaps as a whole class before looking at File 18

Pronunciation

1 Individual, then pairwork comparison.

2 ☐ 37 Listen and allow students to correct their stress patterns then check with the whole class.

> ● • • retailer, dangerous
> • ● • assistant, creative, procedure, consumer
> • • ● engineer, personnel, unemployed
> ● • • • operator, advertising
> • ● • • psychologist, environment, redundancies, economist
> • • ● • occupation, satisfaction, bureaucratic

56

PRESENTATION

> **Optional equipment and materials**
> Handout of jumbled dialogues for Activity 6

1 Warm-up discussion on the problems of travelling – link back to the article on stress in the last unit.

Encourage students to tell anecdotes.

2 [38] Set activity. Point out that students can make notes rather than use full sentences.

Play each conversation straight through once. If students are struggling, play again.

> **a** US entry visa has expired, New York
> **b** Missed connection, Newcastle
> **c** Flight overbooked, Paris

3 [38a] As Student's Book. Remind students that one space represents one word.

> **I** Can I
> **2** you have to
> **3** I can't
> The immigration authorities won't let her in.

4 [38b] As Student's Book.

> She mustn't sit in the smoking section because she's allergic to smoke.
> She doesn't have to do anything about her luggage because the airline will transfer it to the plane for her.

5 [38c] As Student's Book.

> **I** give me that
> **2** there's a seat
> **3** there isn't?
> **4** we have to

6 With a weak class, work through the whole conversation with a good student then set the pairwork. Stop the activity and play 38c again if the pairwork is going badly. With a very weak class, use the following alternative activity.

Number the sentences below and over the page to reconstruct the three dialogues.

> | I |
> | --- |
> | **a** Can I get one in New York? |
> | **b** I'm afraid not. If we take you to New York, the immigration authorities won't let you in. |
> | **c** Is there a problem? |
> | **d** No. You have to apply from outside the USA. |
> | **e** So I can't get on this flight? |
> | **f** Yes. I'm sorry, but your US entry visa has expired |

> | 2 |
> | --- |
> | **a** Good, but I mustn't be in the smoking section. I'm allergic to smoke. |
> | **b** I got in from Toronto late and I've missed my connection to Newcastle. |
> | **c** If there's space, you can have a seat on the next flight. |
> | **d** Thanks. |
> | **e** That's all right. |
> | **f** What about my luggage? |
> | **g** You don't have to do anything about that. We'll transfer it to the plane for you. |

3

a   But I booked last week.

b   Don't worry. We'll get you a seat with another airline if we have to.

c   I'll see if there's a seat.

d   I'm afraid it's overbooked.

e   I'm afraid the whole plane's full. The next flight doesn't arrive till 9.35. Is that too late?

f   I'm very sorry.

g   Look. I must be in Paris by ten. If there's a seat in economy, give me that.

h   No, it's all right.

i   What happens if there isn't?

Practise the conversations in pairs.

Answers to alternative activity

1   a   d   e   b
2   b   c   a   e   f   g   d
3   d   a   f   g   e   h   c   i   b

LANGUAGE WORK

Air Travel

1 Give plenty of time for students to look at the advertisement before asking the questions.

Ask also: *Who asks all these questions? What is the significance of the red flower?*

TWA

White Coats – people who are employed to give information and help to travellers.

Travellers ask these questions.

The White Coats wear them in their buttonholes.

2 Treat this as a two-column matching activity between the first column of the advert and the list in the Student's Book.

1   Is it too early for the bar?
2   Is there anybody here to meet Mrs Leroy?
3   Where can I get a bus into town?
4   Who won last night's ball game?
5   What's the taxi fare to the city centre?
6   Can I go through to the Departure Lounge now?
7   I have to be in Alaska by 8 tonight.
8   What's the code for Cleveland, Ohio?
9   I can't find my boarding card.
10 I have to ring my office.

3 Set a time limit and award points for correct answers. Who's the winner? You could run this and Activity 4 together.

1   a pilot
2   a porter
3   the Duty Free
4   the stopover
5   luggage
6   trolleys
7   the gents
8   on time
9   in time (note the difference between these two)
10 out of date

4 As before, set a time limit and award points for correct answers.

1	boarding	6	to catch
2	declare	7	to rent
3	taking off	8	to check in
4	to reserve	9	going on
5	to cancel	10	please, somebody

5 Pairwork. Students can use the advert or, preferably, make up their own questions here, perhaps for an international airport in the students' own country. The White Coats must invent appropriate answers.

58

Rules and regulations

KEY LANGUAGE POINT: *Must* and *have to* have virtually the same meaning, but *mustn't* is an obligation **not** to do something, whereas *not have to* indicates lack of obligation. There is no form of *must* for Past Simple, Present Perfect or Future, so only forms of *have to* can exist in these cases.

1 Treat this as other activities with a table and an exercise.

> 1 must/have to
> 2 can
> 3 mustn't
> 4 must/have to
> 5 don't have to
> 6 cannot/can't; 'cannot' is more appropriate here because of the level of formality

2 With a weak class go through many if not all of these sentences – students contribute but do not write. Otherwise, demonstrate the first two then set as an individual written activity.

1	don't have to	6	don't have to
2	mustn't	7	don't have to
3	mustn't	8	mustn't
4	don't have to	9	don't have to
5	mustn't	10	don't have to

3 As Student's Book except for pre-experience students.

PX Students can talk about the rules and regulations of the establishment where they are studying. Arrange feedback carefully on the use of these modals.

Get a list of points on the board. Put sentences up even if they are not logical and ask students to challenge them, for example,

Student 1: *We don't have to come late.*
Student 2: *No…We mustn't come late.*

Future possibilities

KEY LANGUAGE POINTS

Conditionals: The three traditional conditional patterns (types 1, 2, and 3) are indeed common, but so are many other patterns. This unit includes type 1 conditionals, along with many other 'open' conditional forms. They are 'open' in the sense that the speaker has an open choice in selecting verb forms. The verbs follow the normal patterns of English and students need only select the tenses that are logical for the situation.

In contrast to the 'open' conditionals in this unit, 'restricted' conditionals will appear later in the book. In these, the speaker's choice of verb forms is restricted and they are less natural, as a past form is often used to express a future idea. So while the traditional type 1 conditional falls into the 'open' category, types 2 and 3 fall into the 'restricted' category. Restricted conditionals are generally reserved for hypothetical situations and students will meet type 2 conditionals in Unit 15. Type 3 conditionals are not covered.

1 This exercise is designed to show a wide variety of open conditional forms. Matching procedure as for two-column activities.

> 1 c 2 l 3 k 4 i 5 h 6 a 7 b 8 d 9 j
> 10 f 11 e 12 g

Draw attention to the many different verb forms used in the *if* clause of these sentences. They include the Present Simple, Present Continuous, Present Perfect, Past Simple, and some modal verbs. Also draw attention to the fact that *will* is not generally used in the same clause as *if*. Instead a Present tense is used to express a future idea. In some other languages it would be possible to use *will* in both clauses.

2 This activity reinforces the fact that within an *if* clause, the Present tense expresses a future idea.

Pairwork. Monitor and encourage students to share some of the best ideas with the whole class.

3 Further practice of the traditional type 1 conditional but with other modals in the second clause – *can*, *could*, etc.

PX Pre-experience students can imagine that the client is visiting their town and therefore take part in the activity.

Pairwork. Monitor as before and provide feedback on some of the best ideas to the whole class.

Pronunciation

1 and **2** 39 This is a minimal pairs activity which reinforces the importance of voicing in English. Practise saying the contrasts in isolation and then put them into the pairs of words. Finally play the cassette to test the students' ability to discriminate. Then put them in pairs to test each other.

In many cases, even native speakers cannot hear these subtle differences in isolation. It is the context which tells them which form is most likely. So do not push it too far. But, on the other hand, recent research suggests that language learners acquire complete features in a language, like voicing, across the whole range of sounds so it is well worth showing how it affects meaning in a range of words such as these.

1	write	4	view
2	prize	5	pack
3	glass		

Company policy

1 and **2** Get students to study the proposals and then suggest what may happen, using the conditional structures already practised. Encourage them to vary the modal forms in the second part of the sentence. Pairwork followed by class discussion and role-play.

PX Pre-experience students could imagine the effects of these proposals on an imaginary company.

Social customs

1 This could be done as a quiz/competition either in pairs or groups or as a whole class activity. You could write each question on a separate card to be used by a 'quiz master'.

2 General discussion. Students write one or more extra questions about a cultural difference foreigners encounter in their country.

SKILLS WORK

Reading

1 This could be done as a high-speed whole-class discussion.

Collect answers on the board to assist students in preparing to attack the text.

Give feedback on some of the major differences students have noticed.

2 As Student's Book. As with all True and False exercises, make sure students can tell you where they found the information which proves or disproves the statement.

1	T	4	F
2	F	5	F
3	F	6	F

60

3 As Student's Book. There is more than one possible
answer for many of these and they are designed to
encourage discussion. Where students disagree with
your choices, ask them to justify theirs.

1	**Greek**	it's a nationality / language not a country.
2	**cow**	it's an animal not a dairy product.
3	**plate**	it's a piece of cutlery not a piece of crockery.
4	**beer**	it's alcoholic.
5	**late**	it's not a kind of milk.
6	**pig**	it's an animal not a meat.
7	**if**	it's not a preposition.
8	**consume**	it's a regular verb, the others are all irregular.
9	**strong**	it does not collocate with 'meal'.
10	**problem**	it's not something you are aiming at.

Speaking

As Student's Book, except pre-experience students.

PX Ask the students to think of some changes they
would like to make to the way the institute they are
studying in is organized. They can choose from (if
applicable):

- the timetabling
- the library system
- the security system
- the self-access centre
- the canteen
- the student car parking
- the syllabus

PRESENTATION

1 Warm up through questions, except pre-experience students.

PX Ask students which companies in their country trade with foreign countries. Ask them to imagine a foreign visitor to one of those companies. What would the visitor want to see in the company?

Teach or elicit: *premises, systems, processes, records, quality control procedures, safety procedures.*

2 As Student's Book.

3 🔲 Set the scene for the listening.

Play the cassette once straight through for the global listening task.

As a variant, do not play the cassette again, even if some students are unsure of their answers. Instead, elicit an answer, play the conversation at that stage, and ask students if the answer is correct.

Ask students which words helped them work out the answer.

> **1** c **2** b **3** a **4** e **5** d

4 🔲 Remind students that one space = one word: this is particularly important here where some of the target words are passives.

After feedback and checking, ask students to practise the extracts from the conversations in pairs.

> **a** are manufactured / is covered
> **b** Have ... ever seen / are put / are taken
> **c** has ... been / Since
> **d** is done / they're paid / They're supplied by ... for
> **e** How long / is taught / has had / since

If students struggled to identify what is going on in the pictures, ask them again to describe the activity in each picture in one sentence.

LANGUAGE WORK

> **Optional equipment and materials**
>
> Index file cards for Systems and processes 1
>
> Large sheets of paper and pens for flowcharts for Systems and processes 5

Achievements

1 As in Student's Book. Encourage students to look at pictures for clues.

2 Do quick vocabulary check on the information. Reverse dictionary or phrase completion, for example,

Teacher: *The company started ... in 1941.*
Students: *trading.*

Ask students to study the example conversation. Write it on the board. Show the difference between *When* and *How long ago* – see board plan.

Some of the questions are quite long. With a strong class, let them struggle. With a weak class, go through the whole activity in class before setting up the pairwork. Ask students to alternate between *How long ago* and *When.*

3 Use the time line on the board to demonstrate the information given in the rubric. Pairwork.

Add the first question above the area bracketed, for example, *How long have AMP been in business?*

With a weak class, you may have to go through all the questions first, as they are not immediately obvious from the information about AMP. Demonstrate on the board that the Present Perfect sentence is linked to the Present Simple sentence, not the past tense action: *AMP started in 1941 – It is in business now – It has been in business for over 50 years.* Link *is* to *has been.*

At this stage, students may try to use any of the following:

> *for* ... period of time
> *since* ... point in time
> *since* ... period of time ... *ago*

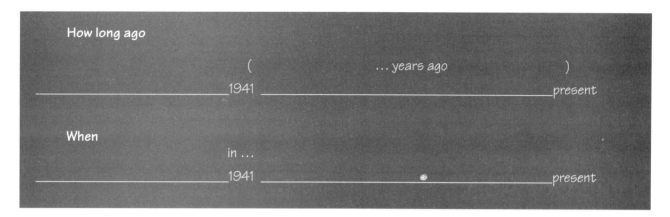

It is probably better if you limit a weaker class to the first option, as the distinction is dealt with later in this unit. It is also good practice in working out and saying in English the difference between a date in the past and the present date, for example, *for 23 years.*

This is not a full explanation of the distinction between the Present Perfect Simple and the Present Perfect Continuous but it is probably enough for students at this level.

4   As Student's Book. Individual written work then pairwork checking.

1	for	**7**	for
2	for	**8**	since
3	since	**9**	for
4	for	**10**	since
5	since	**11**	since
6	since	**12**	since

After students have got the answers in their books, ask them to group the information as below and compare the kinds of words and phrases in each group. This will reinforce the concept of *length of time* vs. *point in time.*

For: 2 days, an hour, a long time, a month, years

Since: Wednesday, last week, 1945, 2 o'clock, yesterday, the 1960s, the stockmarket crash.

With a strong class, show them at this point that we can add *ago* to lengths of time and then say *since, – since 2 days ago.*

Experience

KEY LANGUAGE POINT: The Present Perfect is used in this exercise to talk about things which started in the past and are still true. When students start talking about previous jobs or houses, they must switch to the Past Simple.

1   Pairwork. You may need to teach or elicit suitable answers for people who have only had one job and only lived in one place: *Where have you worked before? – This is my first job. Where have you lived before? – I have always lived in my present house / area.*

Monitor carefully and deal with difficulties such as *What's your present job? – I'm a sales manager. – How long have you had a sales manager?*

PX   By definition, these students cannot do this task. Switch it to talking about their current school or institute and previous ones: where they study (ask *how long*), where they studied before, what their course is, what their previous courses were and so on.

As with students in work, you will need to teach them how to reply if there is no previous experience.

2   Encourage the 'head-hunters / recruiters' to work together to think of the questions they are going to ask. With a strong group, they could go slightly beyond the questions needed to complete the form.

Get the 'managers' to write a brief CV whilst the 'recruiters' are preparing their questions.

Interviews could be one-to-one or panel. As this is a role-play, it is probably better if everyone makes things up. Pre-experience students do not need a separate task. They can invent information.

63

3 KEY LANGUAGE POINT: The Present Perfect is used in this case to ask about experiences in a person's life. The time is not specified in the original question. As soon as the questioner gets a *yes* answer, however, s/he must switch to the Past Simple to talk about the actual experience.

Demonstrate by getting the students to ask you questions. Highlight the change of tense.

Set up pairwork. Monitor and arrange feedback to whole class on the interesting anecdotes.

4 Treat this as a table and exercise. Encourage students to use the information in the note to help them complete the exercise.

1	make	7	make
2	do	8	do
3	make	9	make
4	make	10	do
5	do	11	make
6	make	12	do

As with the *for* and *since* activity above, after students have got the correct answer, ask them to group the information, in this case to highlight the fact that there is practically no logic to the choice – you simply have to learn the collocations.

do: someone a favour, English homework, damage, research, business.

make: a telephone call, a complaint, a decision, a mistake, progress, a profit, enquiries.

5 As Student's Book. Pairwork. Students use Files 17 (page 161) and 25 (page 163). This exercise has two parts. First the students complete the questions and then they must ask and answer them.

Systems and processes

KEY LANGUAGE POINT: The use of the passive in technical writing and description, where the action is of more interest than the agent. With a weak class, revise the form of the passive just before you do the first transformation activity.

1 As Student's Book.

1	is advertised
2	are sorted
3	are discarded
4	are
5	interviewed
6	shortlisted (don't repeat *are*)
7	are analysed
8	are interviewed
9	is made

As an alternative, if you have time, make sets of cards – index file cards are best – which each have one of the stages of the selection process on as follows:

a analysing samples of the candidates' handwriting (graphologist)

b discarding unsuitable applications

c interviewing the candidates again

d interviewing the candidates

e advertising the post

f making the selection

g shortlisting the candidates

h sorting the applications

Give out the cards. Ask students if any parts of the process surprise them – perhaps the use of a graphologist – and explain.

Ask students, working in groups, to put the cards in a logical order to make a selection process. When a group has finished, allow them to look at other groups and compare. Get students to justify their order. Then they can check with the correct order on page 143. Then follow up with Activity 1.

2 As Student's Book.

first	when	next	after that	finally

3 [41] Make sure students realize that you have switched to a new process. Check the concept 'just in time' (only keeping sufficient stock for immediate needs).

Pairwork. Monitor. Do not confirm or correct yet.

Play the cassette for students to check their order.

> 3 7 1 9 5 2 6 8 4

4 Demonstrate with the first two or three sentences on the board. Individual written work – perhaps homework.

> **Possible answer**
>
> First an order is received and fed into the computer. Then the production schedule is arranged. Next the raw materials are taken to the factory floor where the bumpers are manufactured. The bumpers are tested before they are packed in crates. Finally, they are loaded into lorries and delivered to the customers.

5 As Student's Book except for pre-experience students. Give out large sheets of paper for the flow chart if possible or blank OHTs and pens.

PX With an imaginative class you can ask them to imagine a process. Otherwise suggest more mundane things such as: making a cup of tea or coffee, getting into and driving away a car, making a simple meal.

6 As Student's Book. Ideally students should be able to display the flowchart. Small group work.

SKILLS WORK

Writing

1 Ask students to read the advertisement and discuss the first question in pairs. Explain vocabulary as necessary.

Ask students to cover the advertisement. Can they remember the services the company provides?

Prompt them with the verbs:

1 We advise ...
2 We inspect ...
3 We arrange ...
4 We replace ...
5 We service ...
6 We provide ...
7 We deal ...
8 We record ...

2 Demonstrate one sentence only this time, as students have had a lot of practice of constructing the passive. Possible answers:

> 2 Every vehicle is inspected before delivery.
> 3 Signwriting is arranged.
> 4 Tyres, batteries, and exhausts are replaced.
> 5 The vehicles are serviced at any time of the day or night.
> 6 A 24-hour recovery service is provided.
> 7 All the paperwork is dealt with.
> 8 The service history of our customers' fleets is recorded on our computer.

Listening

1 42 Give students time to study the photographs. Ask individual students to describe a photograph and get the other students to guess which they are looking at. But don't pre-teach vocabulary at this stage. Ask students to circumlocute (*A thing to / for ...*). Then proceed to the listening activity.

> 1 Constructing the chassis
> 2 Constructing the car body
> 3 Hanging the doors
> 4 Painting the body
> 5 Fitting the windscreen
> 6 Fitting the mechanical components
> 7 Fitting the wheels
> 8 Testing the brakes
> 9 Testing the car on the track

2 As Student's Book.

65

Pronunciation 43

Once again the focus is on the unpredictability of vowel sounds from the written form. Ask students to read and mark their answers first, then play the cassette for them to check.

1	track	**4**	post
2	step	**5**	worst
3	test	**6**	look

Concentrate on any items that your particular students have special problems with.

Speaking

1, **2** and **3**   As Student's Book except for pre-experience students.

PX   If you feel your students are bored with being stuck with the institute or school as the only location for this type of exercise, suggest outlandish scenarios such as a space station, a bathysphere (deep underwater), or a floating hotel in mid-Atlantic.

PRESENTATION

1 [44] Refer students to the title of the unit and point out that *tackle* in this case means *deal with something difficult*.

Briefly deal with the idea of a 'problem solving process', involving the following stages:

- Identify the problem
- Think of possible solutions
- Evaluate possible solutions
- Choose the best one
- Make the decision

Give plenty of time for students to work out the possible problems of the people in the pictures. (If they correctly identify the problem, ask them for possible solutions.)

Play the cassette once for global questions.

2 As Student's Book. Full answers for the chart are given in 3 below.

3 [44] Play the cassette again for students to complete the chart.

Problem	Possible solutions	Consequences
keys locked in car and must get to the airport quickly	break in	would set off the alarm
	phone for spare set of keys	would be late/ wouldn't arrive at airport on time
	call police for help	they might not be able to open it
	one person takes taxi to airport other stays with car	one person would be there to meet client at airport

4 Demonstrate the structure on the board, showing the relationship with the possible solution.

> 1 They could break into the car. But if they did that, they would set off the alarm.
>
> 2 They could phone for the spare set of keys from the office. If they did that they would be late for the flight at Heathrow.
>
> 3 They could call police for help. If they did that the police might not be able to open the car door.
>
> 4 One person could take a taxi to the airport whilst the other one stays with the car. If they did that then one person would be at the airport on time to meet the client..

Set the activity for pairwork or individual written work.

5 Individual work, then pairwork checking. Play the cassette for a final check.

1	would	6	might
2	could	7	not
3	left	8	Supposing
4	be	9	mean
5	wouldn't		

6 As Student's Book.

LANGUAGE WORK

> **Optional equipment and materials**
> OHT of matching exercise for Negotiating 1

KEY LANGUAGE POINT: The Second Conditional is mainly used to describe the consequences of unlikely actions. Unlike the open conditionals the students met in Unit 13, in the second conditional the verb forms used are restricted and a past verb form is used to express a future idea.

Consequences

1 If this is a new lesson, link back to the last lesson and ask students to try to remember some of the *if* sentences in the problem about the car keys.

General discussion of the questions.

2 Give plenty of time for the reading here – the students may well find some genuinely useful advice! Allow them to use dictionaries.

After ten minutes or so, ask students which suggestions are really useful.

3 Demonstrate the structure again, then elicit ideas from individual students.

Hypothesizing

Although some of these questions relate directly to work, pre-experience students can still take part in this activity as the contexts are all hypothetical or imaginary.

Check closely that students are using *would* correctly in their answers. With a strong class, point out that *might* can also be used if we are not sure of our reactions to these hypothetical situations.

Problems

1 [45] Treat this as a two-column matching activity. Play each of the comments on the cassette, then pause the tape while students search out the appropriate problem.

1 d	**2** e	**3** c	**4** h	**5** b	**6** a	**7** f	**8** g

2 A question for class discussion, except for pre-experience students

Solutions

1 and **2** Point out that this is a new situation. Begin by matching the first two columns (Activity 1). Check the answers, then continue with the third column (Activity 2).

> **1** We're having trouble with one of our customers. They say they can't pay us until next year. We could call in the receivers. But if we did, we'd only get a small part of the money they owe us.
>
> **2** We're having trouble with the prototype for the new model. We could go back to stage one and redesign it. But if we did, our competitors might beat us to the market.
>
> **3** We're having trouble with late deliveries from one of our suppliers. We could take our custom elsewhere. But if we did we would have to pay higher prices.
>
> **4** Someone is stealing small quantities of office supplies. We could search people's bags when they leave the building. But if we did, we might create bad feeling among the staff.
>
> **5** We're having trouble with the chemical treatment plant. It's not big enough. We could dump some of the waste in the river. But if we did, would we poison the surrounding wild life?
>
> **6** We're having trouble with our landlord. He wants to increase the office rents by 30%. We could look for other premises. But if we did, we wouldn't find anywhere as central and convenient as this.

3 As Student's Book.

[PX] If some students in your group are in work and others are not, let the in-work people pose the problems. Pre-experience students can suggest solutions and the in-work people point out the possible consequences. If none of your students are in work, pose a problem yourself which you know to be an issue in your local situation.

Negotiating

1 Check the meaning of the word *negotiate* as it is a false friend in some languages.

With a weak class, ask students to close their books. Introduce the main information through a matching exercise as below – write it on the board or use an OHT. On the left are some of the main elements in any terms of sale. Match each example on the right with the term it represents.

1 Price	**a**	5%	
2 Credit Period	**b**	500 pieces	
3 Delivery time	**c**	$65 per piece	
4 Minimum order	**d**	50% if less than 4 weeks before delivery	
5 Discount	**e**	30 days	
6 Cancellation penalty	**f**	8 weeks	

> ***Answers to alternative activity***
> **1** c **2** e **3** f **4** b **5** a **6** d

Refer students to the table in the Student's Book to check their answers. With a strong class, continue as Student's Book. With a weak class, do a high-speed oral-matching exercise before the pairwork. Ask the students to match the complaint to the term or terms which could be complained about, for example:

> **a** That's rather short. 2
> **b** That's rather long. 3
> **c** That's rather large. 4
> **d** that's rather low. 5
> **e** That's rather high. 1, 6

rather in this case means *more than I wanted* or *expected*; *quite*, on the other hand, would mean *a little* or *very* in AmE.

2 As Student's Book.

3 A highly-controlled speaking activity. Focus on the form as much as on the fluency. Pairwork.

4 Still highly controlled. Point out that we can use the Second Conditional to suggest a compromise.

Give weaker students the following situation: A customer is buying some office furniture from a supplier. Then say the statements below and ask students to decide who could say them – the customer (C), the supplier (S) or either (C/S).

We'd like you to...

1 *increase the discount.*
2 *pay in dollars.*
3 *pay for delivery.*
4 *pay for installation.*
5 *reduce the price.*
6 *accept a penalty clause for cancellation.*
7 *accept a penalty clause for late delivery.*
8 *pay by letter of credit.*
9 *install it over the weekend.*
10 *let us use your offices as a showroom for our customers.*

> **1** C **2** S **3** C/S **4** C/S **5** C **6** S
> **7** C **8** S **9** C **10** S

Reset the whole situation and divide students into two groups – customers and suppliers. Customers and suppliers work out their 'bottom line' in secret.

Role-play the negotiations. Focus now is on fluency rather than total accuracy.

SKILLS WORK

> **Optional equipment and materials**
> OHT blank of chart for Listening 1

Listening

1 ▭ 46 Be prepared to play the cassette several times, perhaps focusing on different 'columns' each time: first play = subject, second = head office wants.

Provide feedback after each playing on to board – or OHT if possible. Possible answers, see table below.

2 Play the cassette again if necessary. The misunderstanding is quite subtle. Try to get students to disentangle it completely.

> The Sales Office thought the Head Office meant they would pay for 4 days a month because it takes one person one day each week to compile them. Head Office thought they only needed one day's work a month.

3 ▭ 46a Refer students to the conversation plan whilst they listen to the first part of the conversation again. Demonstrate use of conversation plan with a good student. Then set for pairwork.

4 ▭ 46b Give students time to read the questions before playing the second part of the conversation.

> **1** They base the calculations of the sales targets on last year's sales.
> **2** They had a large order from the Ministry of Defence, which was unusual.
> **3** 'It's company policy. We always insist on this.'

5 ▭ 46c As Student's Book.

> Could we go through it again and check what we've agreed?
>
> You're going to send us your sales figures every <u>week</u>.
>
> And you're going to pay for <u>four</u> days' secretarial help each month.
>
> No. We agreed to pay for <u>one</u> day.

Point out that the main stress falls on the word that carries important information.

	Part 1	*Part 2*	*Part 3*
The subject of discussion	sales statistic	sales targets	what they've agreed
What the head office wants	sales statistics evey week	targets based on last year's sales figures	to pay for one day's help per month
What the sales office wants	an extra day's secretarial help	lower targets	four days' help a month
Do they agree on a compromise?	Yes	No	No

Pronunciation

Sentence stress does not normally convey a lot of meaning but it does in some special cases. Link this to the last activity above.

1 [47]   As Student's Book.

> **1** I didn't say we would pay you five hundred <u>pounds</u>.
>
> **2** I didn't say <u>we</u> would pay you five hundred pounds.
>
> **3** I didn't say we would <u>pay</u> you five hundred pounds.
>
> **4** <u>I</u> didn't say we would pay you five hundred pounds.
>
> **5** I didn't say we <u>would</u> pay you five hundred pounds.
>
> **6** I didn't say we would pay you <u>five</u> hundred pounds.
>
> **7** I didn't say we would pay <u>you</u> five hundred pounds.

2 [47]   As Student's Book.

> **1** d   **2** f   **3** c   **4** b   **5** g   **6** a   **7** e

3 As Student's Book. Pairwork.

Speaking 1

Pairwork or small groups.

As Student's Book except with weaker students. For weaker students, do this matching exercise first.

Read the situations and decide which of the following compromises fits each situation:

a If you covered the cost of postage and packaging, we would pay for the translation.

b If you paid the fees, the employees would be prepared to come in their own time.

c If you reduced the length, we would be able to come.

d If you increased the staff discount, they would be more attractive.

e If you paid it, we would offer a one-year warranty.

> **1** e   **2** d   **3** c   **4** b   **5** a

Now ask students to think of a compromise for the one missing – i.e. 6. Then revert to Speaking 1.

Speaking 2

1–4 General discussion to round off the course.

Test 1 | Units 1–3

1 Company information   10 marks

Put the verb in brackets into the Present Simple tense, as in the example.

What company __do__ you __work__ for? (work)

1   It's a high tech company. It _____ a lot of money in research and development. (invest)

2   I _____ based in Chicago. (be)

3   Is it a big company? How many people _____ it _____ ? (employ)

4   Which division _____ you _____ in? (work)

5   They _____ a high quality service. (provide)

6   They _____ _____ any products in Chicago. (not manufacture)

7   It's a Japanese company. The Head Office _____ in Tokyo. (be)

8   It _____ _____ a sales representative in Thailand. (not have)

9   Luca Ceresa _____ in the Research Division. (work)

10 _____ the offices open on Saturday? (be)

2 Current activities   10 marks

Put the verb in brackets into the Present Continuous tense, as in the example.

We __are expanding__ our sales team at the moment. (expand)

1   How many new staff _____ you _____ _____ (take on)?

2   My boss _____ _____ arrangements to interview 250 applicants. (make)

3   At the moment, I _____ _____ a new system to monitor and track applications. (introduce)

4   Someone else _____ _____ all the interviews. (organize)

5   _____ you _____ to expand the marketing team too? (plan)

3 Jobs and responsibilities   5 marks

Put the words in the right order to make questions.

1   Peter in department which work does ?

   _____

   _____

© Oxford University Press   PHOTOCOPIABLE

2 who report you to do ?

_____

_____

3 are project you on which working ?

_____

_____

4 do do living what for you a ?

_____

_____

5 responsible who recruiting staff is for new ?

_____

_____

4 Personal profile   10 marks

Choose the correct words in *italics* to complete this article.

Sir David Simon is chairman of BP, Britain's biggest oil company. BP *employs/is employing* 60,000 people worldwide, and it *changes/is changing* under his chairmanship. It *looks/is looking* for new opportunities abroad and *becomes/is becoming* more profitable. BP is involved in an exciting new venture in Algeria at the moment. It *starts/is starting* a new drilling project in the Sahara desert.

Sir David usually *spends/is spending* around four days a week on BP business and he *holds/is holding* a number of executive positions with other companies.

Outside work, Sir David *plays/is playing* golf, *watches/is watching* Arsenal football team and *enjoys/is enjoying* going to the opera.

5 Facilities   10 marks

Read the information about training centre facilities, then complete the conversations.

Use these words: *there is, it is, there are, they are.*

TRAINING CENTRE FACILITIES

Fax machines
Room L352 and L379 (1 in each room)
Resource Centre(2)

Photocopiers
Room L321 (1 model ZX94 and 2 model ZX 994s)

Overhead Projectors
Additional projectors available in Resource Centre

Coffee machine
Ground floor lobby

1 _____ _____ any fax machines?

Yes, _____ _____ four.

Where _____ _____ ?

_____ _____ one in Room L352

and _____ _____ two in the

Resource Centre.

2 _____ _____ a coffee machine?

Yes, _____ _____ in the ground

floor lobby.

3 Where are the ZX 994 photocopiers?

_____ _____ in Room 321.

4 _____ _____ a ZX94

photocopier?

Yes, _____ _____

6 Greetings and introductions   10 marks

Complete these conversations with a suitable word or phrase.

1 **Jon**   Hello, Pietro. It's nice to see you again.

    How _____ ?

   Pietro   Fine thanks, and you?

   Jon   _____

2 **Berndt**   Luigi, _____ introduce

    you to Lisa Parks? Luigi,

    _____ Lisa.

   Luigi   How _____ ?

   Lisa   Nice _____

   Berndt   Lisa works in our Plastics Division. She's

    in _____ of Research.

3 **Secretary** Good morning. Can I

    _____ ?

   Visitor Yes, my name is Jorge Castano and I

    _____ an appointment

    to see Miss Fenton at eleven o'clock.

   Secretary Please take a seat Mr Castano and

    _____ you're here.

7 Telephoning   15 marks

Complete these conversations. Use one word in each space.

1 **Pierre**   Customer services, good afternoon.

   Lee   I'd _____ to speak to Mrs Scott,

    please.

   Pierre   Who's _____ , please?

   Lee   Lee Sang Yop.

   Pierre   One moment, Mr Lee, I'll put you

    _____ .

2 **Pierre**   Customer Services, good afternoon.

   Emma   Hello. Could I speak to Mrs Scott,

    _____ ?

   Pierre   I'm _____ she's on the other line

    at the moment. Will you _____ ,

    or can I take a _____ ?

   Emma   No, I'll call _____ later, thanks.

3 **Pierre**   Customer Services, good afternoon.

   Marcus   Could I speak to Pierre, please?

   Pierre   _____ .

   Marcus   Oh hello Pierre. _____ is Marcus.

    I'm phoning about our order.

4 **Pierre**   Customer services, good afternoon.

   Rosa   Jane Parks, please.

   Pierre   I'm afraid she's not here just now.

   Rosa   Could you _____ her a message?

   Pierre   Yes, of _____ Hold

    _____ , _____ get a

    pencil. OK, go _____ .

   Rosa   Could you ask her to call me? My number

    is 01799 524 153.

8 Spot the mistake 20 marks

There is one mistake in every sentence. Find the mistake and correct it.

1 Can I introduce you to Mr Takeuchi? He's engineer in our Osaka plant.

2 How many subsidiaries does your company have got?

3 If you want to make a copy, it's a photocopier in the next room.

4 The Research Division recruits more staff at the moment.

5 He speaks to someone on the other line right now.

6 'Who's speaking?' 'Here is Inge Russ.'

7 Have you met Edward Hanson? He's the responsible for new markets.

8 I'm afraid but he can't speak to you at the moment. Can I take a message?

9 Do you want to speak to Pilar? I call her.

10 He is usually playing tennis in his free time.

9 Vocabulary quiz 10 marks

1 The main office of a company is its

h _____ . (12)

2 Do I have to pay now or can you i_____ me later? (7)

3 IT means Information T._____ . (10)

4 The total sales of a company is its

t_____ (8).

5 A company with subsidiaries in many countries is a

m_____ . (13)

6 The opposite of formal is i_____ . (8)

7 The P_____ Department recruits new employees. (9)

8 She is responsible _____ sales. (3)

9 She reports _____ the Marketing Director. (2)

10 The people who work for a company are its

e_____ . (9)

1   Yesterday   10 marks

Complete the conversation. Use *was, were, wasn't* or *weren't*.

A   Where _____ you yesterday?

B   At work. I rang you but you _____ in.

A   I _____ in London. There _____ a meeting about the new distribution system. Why _____ you there?

B   I didn't know it about it.

A   The new project manager wanted to speak to you. She _____ very pleased when she found out you _____ there. Didn't you see the e-mail about it?

B   No. Who else _____ there?

A   Everyone. Why didn't you read your e-mail?

B   I _____ too busy. I thought it _____ important.

2   Asking questions   5 marks

Put the words in the right order to make questions.

1   like what conference the was ?

_____

_____

2   the last how did conference long ?

_____

_____

3   like were what facilities the ?

_____

_____

4   interesting presentations were very the ?

_____

_____

5   attended how your people many presentation ?

_____

_____

3   Size and dimension   10 marks

Read the information about computer hardware, then complete the questions and answers.

Apple Macintosh, Performa 6200 System

	Weight	Height	Width	Length
CPU	8.6 kg	10.9 cm	32 cm	41.9 cm
Keyboard	250 gm	2.5 cm	14.2 cm	41 cm
Mouse	15 gm	2.75 cm	6 cm	10.3 cm

1   What is the _____ of the CPU?

    It's 10.9 cm _____ .

2   How _____ is the CPU?

    It _____ 8.6 kg.

3   What is the _____ of the mouse?

It's 6 cm _____ .

4   How _____ is the mouse?

It's 10.3 cm _____ .

5   How much does the keyboard _____ ?

The _____ of the keyboard is 250 gm.

4 Company history   10 marks

Make questions about the history of BASF. First read the answers, then complete the questions, as in the example.

When _did BASF start trading in Germany?_

It started trading in Germany in 1865.

1   What happened _____

_____ ?

BASF began industrial-scale production of polystyrene in 1930.

2   When _____

_____ ?

It launched its famous magnetic tape in 1935.

3   What division _____

_____ ?

It established a pharmaceutical division in 1968.

4   Where _____

_____ in 1989?

It opened an environmental control centre in Ludwigshafen, Germany.

5   Which anniversary _____

_____ in 1995?

It celebrated its 25th anniversary.

5 Vocabulary quiz   10 marks

The first letter of each word is provided.

1   The opposite of comfortable is

u_____ . (13)

2   The opposite of efficient is i_____ (11).

3   'What s_____ is it?' 'It's rectangular.' (5)

4   Many small shops are closing because of

c_____ from supermarkets. (11)

5   It's easy to raise or lower this chair; the height is

a_____ . (10)

6   Before we go ahead with this project we should run

a f_____ study. (11)

7   Cauliflower, peas and onions are all

v_____ . (10)

8   A b_____ is a book about someone's

life. (9)

9   You play squash, but you _____ jogging and you

_____ aerobics. (2/2)

6 Saying when   10 marks

Complete the phrases. Use *at*, *in* or *on*.

1 _____ 1989

2 _____ March

3 _____ the beginning of the month

4 _____ Tuesday

5 _____ Christmas

6 _____ 22 May 1997

7 _____ midday

8 _____ Thursday afternoon

9 _____ two-thirty

10 _____ the morning

7 Spot the mistake   20 marks

Find and correct the mistake in each sentence.

1 What was like your vacation?

2 We were all very boring during his presentation.

3 It's a pen you use for to write on OHTs.

4 You learn by doing mistakes.

5 Where you went on your last business trip?

6 When did start the new system?

7 He arrived here on last Monday.

8 I'd like some piece of chicken, please.

9 I usually play squash one time a week.

10 What means 'selective'?

8 Social English   10 marks

Match these phrases with the right answers below.

1 Is this your first visit to Oxford?

2 Is there a good restaurant near here?

3 What would you like to drink?

4 How do you do?

5 Thank you.

6 I'm very sorry.

7 How are you?

8 How often do you travel on business?

9 Would you like fish or meat?

10 Would you like a biscuit?

a No. I'm afraid there isn't.

b Thanks, I'd love one.

c I think I'll have the salmon.

d I'm fine thanks and you?

e I'll just have mineral water, please.

f No, it isn't. I came on holiday last year.

g It doesn't matter.

h How do you do?

i About twice a year.

j Don't mention it.

9 Past developments   15 marks

Complete this story about the development of the internet. Use the past form of the verbs in brackets.

The History Of The Internet

In 1957 the Soviet Union _____ (launch) the first satellite, Sputnik, into space. In response, the US government _____ (set up) the Advanced Research Projects Agency – ARPA – to research and develop new technologies.

By the mid 1960s, there _____ (be) a large amount of sensitive information stored at ARPA and the government _____ (become) concerned about the possibility of nuclear war. It _____ (think) a network of small computers would be more difficult to destroy than one supercomputer so in 1969 it _____ (establish) ARPA net to develop systems for linking computers. Universities and other research institutions soon _____ (get) involved and the network _____ (grow) fast.

In the 1980s, the National Science Foundation – NSF – _____ (develop) a network which _____ (link) five university super computers. This _____ (create) new high speed connections, and people all over the world _____ (be) able to access the net.

Between 1984 and 1988 the number of host computers _____ (rise) from 1,000 to 60,000. In 1990 the US government _____ (transfer) complete control of the net to the NSF. Before long the net _____ (have) more than 6 million host computers.

1 A meeting   10 marks

Complete the conversation. Use the phrases below.

do you feel   *that's a good idea*   *we need to discuss*
be responsible for this   *think we should*
do you think   *I disagree*   *why don't*   *I don't think*
shall we

Marc   OK. As you know, several new projects are

beginning soon. _____ how

to staff them. I _____

outsource a lot of the work. How _____

_____ about that Claire?

Claire   _____ . If we outsource the

work, we lose control. What

_____ , Pete?

Pete   I'm afraid we need to outsource the work.

_____ we have enough staff

for all the projects.

Claire   I see.

Pete   _____ we find out what

people are available? _____

contact an agency?

Marc   _____ . Then we can work

out the costs and establish a control system. Is

that OK with you, Claire?

Claire   OK, but who is going to _____

_____ ?

2 Giving reasons   5 marks

Complete the sentences. Use the correct form of
the verb to be with *going to* or *not going to*.

We __*are not going to*__ drive to the meeting because

there's a good train service.

1 I _____ invest a lot of money in this

project because I think it will be very successful.

2 He _____ send them a letter

because it takes too long.

3 We _____ take on more staff

because the Christmas period is always very busy.

4 I _____ visit Head Office next week

because the meeting is cancelled.

5 You _____ to be surprised when

you hear the news.

3 Plans and arrangements   5 marks

Put the words in the right order to make questions.

1 Peter seeing you when are ?

_____

_____

2 begin time conference what the does ?

_____

_____

3 he tomorrow arriving is morning ?

_____

_____

4 London the to next when plane does leave ?

_____

_____

5 your are new when job going you to start ?

_____

_____

4 **Arrangements**   20 marks

Read the diary notes about a business trip and
complete the answers to the questions.

TUESDAY
7.40   Flight BA902 to Frankfurt. Arrives 10.15
1.30 pm   Josh Kaminski
8 pm   Dinner Zum Goldfinger

WEDNESDAY
9.30 am - 5.00 pm   Seminar
                    My presentation – 12.30
8 pm   Dinner with Christian and Uli

THURSDAY
am   Head Office
15.30   Flight BA905 to London. Arrives 16.05

I What time does her flight to Frankfurt leave?

It _____

_____

2 When does the seminar begin on Wednesday?

It _____

_____

3 When is she meeting Josh Kaminski?

She _____

_____

4 What's she doing on Wednesday evening?

She _____

_____

5 Where is she going on Thursday morning?

She _____

_____

Now write the questions for these answers.

6 _____

_____ ?

She arrives in Frankfurt at 10.15.

7 _____

_____ ?

She's having dinner at Zum Goldfinger.

8 _____

_____ ?

At 12.30 on Wednesday.

9 _____

_____ ?

At 3.30 on Thursday afternoon.

10 _____

_____ ?

It arrives at 16.05.

5 Invitations   10 marks

Put the conversation in the correct order. Number the boxes.

☐ In the city centre. Opposite the station.

☐ Nothing special. Why?

☐ That's a good idea. Where are you going?

☐ Oh, I know the place. What time?

☐ Great. See you there, then.

☐ Michel's Restaurant. Do you know it?

☐ I'm meeting Jo for dinner. How about joining us?

☐ What are you doing on Friday evening?

☐ No. Where is it?

☐ 8 o'clock.

6 Making appointments   10 marks

Complete the conversation. Use one word in each space.

A Could we fix a time to meet? Are you

_____ on Thursday?

B No, I'm _____ , I'm _____ up all

day on Thursday. _____ about Friday?

A Yes, Friday suits me. What time would be

_____ for you?

B Can you _____ 10.30?

A Yes, 10.30's _____ .

B Good. I'll look _____ to _____

you at 10.30 on Friday, _____ .

7 Spot the mistake   20 marks

There is one mistake in every line. Find the mistake and correct it.

1   We should to leave work early this evening.

2   Why we don't play squash this afternoon?

3   Why they are going to take on new staff?

4   When your flight leaves?

5   Our supplier's prices increased at 7% last month.

6   How about to come to the cinema this evening?

7   'We need a new computer system.' 'I am agree.'

8   I'm not think we should buy this new laser printer.

9   Tim was not agree with the proposal.

10 Would you like going to that new Italian bar?

8 Trends   10 marks

This graph shows the market share of TV channels in Britain. Complete the sentences using words and phrases below.

rose   remained steady   by   fell sharply   to
at   of   went   from   recovered slightly

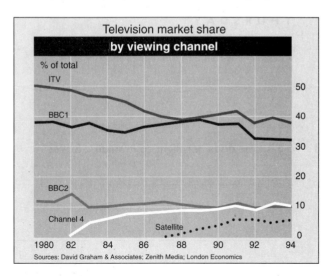

1 ITV's market share _____ _____ between 1980 and 1988.

2 It _____ _____ in 1991, but fell again in 1992.

3 Between 1980 and 1994 it decreased _____ 50% _____ about 37%.

4 In the same period, BBC1's share of the market also _____ down. It fell _____ around 5%.

5 BBC2's market share _____ _____ between 1980 and 1994. It stayed _____ about 10%.

6 Channel 4 started broadcasting in 1982. Between '82 and '94 its share _____ to around 10%.

7 Satellite channels started broadcasting in 1987 and after a slow start, they achieved a market share _____ about 8% in 1994.

9 **Vocabulary quiz**   10 marks

Choose the correct words in italics.

1 We *lent/borrowed* a lot of money from the bank last year.

2 Prices increased *by/at* 2.3% last year.

3 We spend too much money *on/in* advertising and promotion.

4 Our market share increased *dramatic/dramatically* last year.

5 Our poor performance last year was *due to/resulted to* increased competition.

6 There was a sharp increase *on/in* sales last year.

7 This graph shows our sales *numbers/figures* for the past year.

8 Can we *cancel/postpone* our meeting until next week, please?

9 We hope to achieve a *steady/steadily* growth in sales.

10 Salaries *fell/felt* by a small amount last year.

1 **Recent achievements**   10 marks

Complete the article using the Present Perfect form of the verb in brackets, as in the example.

> ### NERA Transmits
> ### Positive Signals
>
> Nera, Norway's specialist telecommunications manufacturer, _has expanded_ (expand) rapidly in recent years. It _____ (achieve) a 34% market share and _____ (become) the market leader, ahead of NEC at 15%.
>
> Once part of the Swedish-Swiss multinational ABB, NERA _____ (be) quoted on the Oslo stock exchange since January 1995. Sales _____ (increase) sharply in recent years and it _____ (build) up a record order book. The company's revenues _____ (grow) by 20% since 1987 and orders in key areas _____ (show) strong growth. Pre-tax profits _____ (rise) dramatically. Much of its growth _____ (result) from its Saturn Miniphone, a lightweight global satellite phone. Only orders for land-earth stations _____ (fall), but this sector is expected to recover in the near future.

2 **Performance**   5 marks

Put the words in the right order to make questions.

1 sales have performance you improved your ?

_____

_____

2 best which results division achieved has the ?

_____

_____

3 its division has your exceeded target ?

_____

_____

4 targets all divisions achieved have their the ?

_____

_____

5 your how turnover has much this increased year ?

_____

_____

3 Checking progress   15 marks

Imagine this is your job list. You have ticked the jobs you have done. Write questions and answers, as in the example.

> **THINGS TO DO** (Thursday)
>
> 1 Take leaflets to printers
> 2 Check the flight times ✔
> 3 Book ticket to Paris ✔
> 4 Ring Pete Burns
> 5 Arrange meeting with Donald – 10.30 Friday ✔
> 6 Write sales report

Your boss   _Have you taken the leaflets to the_
printers yet? (leaflets)

You   _No, I haven't._

1 Your boss _____
_____ ? (flight)

You _____

2 Your boss _____
_____ ? (ticket)

You _____

3 Your boss _____
_____ ? (Pete)

You _____

4 Your boss _____
_____ ? (meeting)

You _____

5 Your boss _____
_____ ? (report)

You _____

4 Quantity   10 marks

Complete the sentences. Use *much* or *many*.

1 Unfortunately, the consultant couldn't give me
_____ advice.

2 The consultant didn't make _____
suggestions, but they were all useful.

3 They suggested that when I didn't have
_____ work, I used my time
to plan ahead.

4 How _____ times have you seen him?

5 How _____ jobs have you done?

6 How _____ experience have you got of
this type of work?

7 Have you done _____ research in
this field?

8 Have they invested in _____ new
machines?

9 Why do they need so _____ new
equipment?

10 He gave us lots of opinions, but not
_____ facts.

5 Giving advice   5 marks

Match the following statements with the advice below.

1 I'm late for my appointment.

2 I haven't had a reply to my letter.

3 We need some cartridges for the printers.

4 I haven't got time to deal with my correspondence.

5 I think we should discuss the new project.

a You'd better arrange a meeting.

b You'd better let them know.

c You'd better take on a temporary secretary.

d You'd better order some.

e You'd better check if they've received it.

6 Predictions   5 marks

Unemployment	This month's rate	Forecast for next month
Austria	4.7%	4.7%
Denmark	9.8%	9.5%
France	11.5%	11.5%
Norway	4.6%	5.0%
Spain	15.4%	15.4%
Switzerland	4.0%	4.2%

Look at the forecasts for unemployment rates in different countries. Make predictions using *will* or *won't* and the words given, as in the example.

increase/Austria   *Unemployment won't increase*
   in Austria.

1 go up/Denmark _____

   _____

2 fall/France _____

   _____

3 rise/Norway _____

   _____

4 remain steady/Spain _____

   _____

5 decrease/Switzerland _____

   _____

7 Comparisons   20 marks

Complete this conversation. Use the correct form of the adjective in brackets to make comparisons, as in the examples.

Our prices are *the cheapest* (cheap) in town.

Formatted disks are *more expensive* (expensive) than the standard ones.

A I'd like some computer disks, please.

B Standard or formatted?

A What's the difference?

B Formatted disks are _____ (convenient).

   You have to format the standard disks yourself so it

   takes _____ (long).

A OK, I'll have the formatted.

B Double or high density?

A Which are _____ (good)?

B You can store more information on the high density.

A OK. I'll have high density then.

B What make would you like?

A What makes do you have?

B Several. 3M is _____ (popular) brand we sell, but their disks are also _____ (expensive). We also sell Verbatim. Their discs are _____ (cheap) than 3Ms, but _____ (expensive) than ours. Our own brand is _____ (cheap).

A Which ones are _____ (reliable)?

B 3M's come with a lifetime guarantee. But Verbatim's disks are all tested. We issue a quality certificate with ours.

A OK, so which of the three is _____ (good) value?

8 Spot the mistake   20 marks

There is one mistake in every line. Find the mistake and correct it.

1 So far this year, we are very busy.

2 We have achieved all our sales targets last year.

3 Can you help me? I need some informations.

4 Can you hurry up, please? I haven't got many time.

5 I'll tell Peter the news when I will see him.

6 You'd better not to go now; go tomorrow instead.

7 Shall I to help you?

8 We expect increase our sales next year.

9 Own-brand products are more cheap than brand-name goods.

10 Of all the products on the market, you'll find theirs is the expensive.

9 Vocabulary quiz   10 marks

1 His sales t_____ (6) was 3,000 units but he only sold 2,500. He didn't achieve it.

2 Some people employ a s_____ (11) to buy and sell shares.

3 Last year, no shareholders received any money; the company didn't pay a d_____ . (8)

4 The age of r_____ (10) for men is 65.

5 I'm leaving my job; I'm going to r_____ (6)

6 When there's an increase in the money supply, the rate of i_____ (9) rises.

7 We can't find the staff we need. There's a s_____ (8) of well-qualified applicants.

8 We had to make 350 staff r_____ (9) due to the recession.

9 How much profit will we make? What's our m_____ ? (6)

10 Which is the odd one out: *dismiss, sack, or recruit?*

1 Company rules   10 marks

Complete these sentences about a company's regulations. Use *must*, *mustn't* or *don't have to*.

1   We operate a no-smoking policy. That means you
    _____ smoke anywhere in the building.

2   We have a flexi-time system – you choose your own

    hours, but you _____ be at work during

    the core time of 10.30 to 15.30. You

    _____ get to work until 10.30, if you like,

    but you _____ leave work before 15.30.

    Outside core time, you _____ keep the

    same hours every day; you can vary them as much as

    you like.

3   Please make sure your visitors know about our strict

    security policy. All visitors _____ report

    to Reception and wait for their host to collect them.

    Visitors' badges _____ be worn at all

    times; visitors _____ walk around the

    building without a badge.

4   We have a clean desk policy. You _____

    leave any papers on your desk when you leave the

    building; if you do, they will be destroyed.

5   We prefer you to take your holiday within a

    calendar year, but you _____ . You can

    transfer up to two weeks to the following year.

2 If …   10 marks

Match the two halves of these sentences.

1   If we offered you the job, …

2   If I need any help, …

3   If his references are OK, …

4   If you don't like the terms and conditions, …

5   If the printer breaks down, …

6   If you have time, …

7   If I have a beer at lunch time, …

8   If you meet the deadlines …

9   If he stopped complaining all the time, …

10 If I spoke better English, …

a   we won't fall behind schedule.

b   we'll offer him the job.

c   I'll show you round the factory.

d   I might get promoted.

e   we call maintenance.

f   when would you be able to start?

g   he'd be much nicer to work with.

h   I'll contact you.

i   don't sign the contract.

j   I feel sleepy all afternoon.

3 Possibilities   10 marks

Choose the correct word or words in italics.

1 Be careful! If you *drop/will drop* it, you

   damage/will damage it.

2 If I *will hear/hear* any more news, I *tell/will tell* you.

3 Please tell Liz I called, if you *see/will see* her.

4 If I *don't finish/won't finish* this tonight,

   I *miss/will miss* the deadline.

5 What happens if you *open/will open* this door?

6 I *give/will give* him your message if he *rings/will ring*

   this afternoon.

4 How long   10 marks

Complete the phrases. Use *since* or *for*.

1 _____ Thursday

2 _____ a week

3 _____ ages

4 _____ he started work

5 _____ three weeks

6 _____ last year

7 _____ a few minutes

8 _____ 1990

9 _____ September

10 _____ some time

5 Career history   10 marks

Read this extract from an accountant's CV, then complete the questions, as in the examples.

1985	Qualified as an accountant
1985–88	Erith Plastics, New York
1988–91	Rovotec, Perth, Australia
1991– the present	Rovotec, London, UK

When (join) *did she join* Erith Plastics?

How long *has she lived* (live) in London?

1 How long _____ (be) an accountant?

2 When _____ (become) an accountant?

3 How long _____ (work) for Erith

   Plastics?

4 How long _____ (work) in the UK?

5 When _____ (join) Rovotec?

6 How long _____ (work) for Rovotec?

7 How long _____ (live) in Australia?

8 When _____ (move) to London?

9 How many jobs _____ (have) since

   1985?

10 How many times _____ (change) jobs?

6 Experiences   10 marks

Choose the correct word or words in italics.

1   *I've never broken/I never broke* my leg, but

    I've broken/I broke my arm last year. It was on a skiing

    holiday. I had to sit and watch everybody else skiing

    for ten days!

2   He *has been learning/learned* to drive since 1990, but

    he *hasn't passed/didn't pass* his driving test yet.

    He's had over 200 lessons.

3   *I've worked/I worked* for three different companies

    since I left college, but *I haven't worked/I never worked*

    overseas.

4   *Have you ever used/Did you ever use* multi-media

    during a training course? I *have/did.* It was very

    useful.

5   *I have had to/had to* give a lot of presentations since

    I took this job, but I *haven't given/didn't give* one in a

    foreign language.

7 Safety procedure   10 marks

Put the verbs in brackets into the correct passive
form, as in the examples.

The buildings *are inspected* (inspect) regularly by the

Fire Officer.

All electrical equipment *is checked* (check) every

two weeks.

FIRE REGULATIONS

When a fire _____ (discover), the alarm

_____ (sound) and fire doors

_____ (close) automatically. As soon as the

alarm goes off, employees _____ (require)

to leave the building by the nearest exit, and to proceed

to the assembly point. The Fire Brigade

_____ (contact) automatically, and

employees _____ (request) to wait until

they _____ (tell) it is safe to return to the

building. Fire drills _____ (conduct)

regularly to ensure everyone is familiar with the

system. All employees _____ (oblige) to

take part and records _____ (keep) by the

Fire Officer.

8 Spot the mistake   20 marks

There is one mistake in every line. Find the mistake
and correct it.

1   If you will have a problem, please let me know.

2   I'm very sorry but I can't to leave yet.

3   I have been here since three weeks.

4   Tim has never went to Africa.

5   What time have you arrived this morning?

6   I am working with BP since 1990.

7   Where are manufactured Swatch watches?

8   The circuit boards assemble on this part of the line.

9   I don't get enough time to make my homework.

10 If you would leave now, you would catch the train.

9 Vocabulary quiz   10 marks

Use one word in each space.

1   They've accepted more reservations than the
    number of seats on the plane. The flight is
    o_____ . (10)

2   Are you travelling first class, business (or club)
    class, or e_____ (7) class?

3   You can't buy the ticket when you get there; you
    have to book in a_____ . (7)

4   The company went p_____ (6) in 1995
    and its shares were listed on the London stock
    exchange.

5   Our stocks of materials are too large. We need to
    reduce our i_____ . (9)

6   If they won't reduce the price, we'll take our
    c_____ (6) elsewhere.

7   He wanted us to give him a r_____ (6)
    (his money back).

8   If you pay cash, we will give you
    a d_____ . (8)

9   We spend too much on rent, heat, light, salaries
    etc. We need to reduce our o_____ .(9)

10 There was a one year guarantee but the suppliers
    agreed to e_____ (6) it to two years.

Answers

TEST 1

1 Company information 10 marks

1 invests
2 am
3 does, employ
4 do, work
5 provide
6 don't manufacture
7 is
8 doesn't have
9 works
10 are

2 Current activities 10 marks

1 are, taking on
2 is making
3 am introducing
4 is organizing
5 are, planning

3 Jobs and responsibilities 5 marks

1 Which department does Peter work in?
2 Who do you report to?
3 Which project are you working on?
4 What do you do for a living?
5 Who is responsible for recruiting new staff?

4 Personal profile 10 marks

employs, is changing, is looking, is becoming, is starting, spends, holds, plays, watches, enjoys

5 Facilities 10 marks

1 Are there, there are, are they, There is, there are
2 Is there, it is
3 They are
4 Is there, there is

6 Greetings and introductions
10 marks

1 are you, Fine thanks/Not so bad thanks
2 May I, this is, do you do, to meet you, charge
3 help you, have, I'll tell her

7 Telephoning 15 marks

1 like, speaking, through
2 please, afraid, hold, message, back
3 Speaking, This
4 give, course, on, I'll, ahead

8 Spot the mistake 20 marks

1 … an engineer …
2 … does your company have / has your company got?
3 … there's a photocopier …
4 … is recruiting …
5 … is speaking …
6 Inge Russ / This is Inge Russ.
7 He's responsible for …
8 I'm afraid he can't …
9 I'll call her.
10 He usually plays …

9 Vocabulary quiz 10 marks

1 headquarters
2 invoice
3 technology
4 turnover
5 multinational
6 informal
7 Personnel
8 for
9 to
10 employees

TEST 2

1 Yesterday 10 marks

were, weren't, was, was, weren't, wasn't, weren't, was, was, wasn't

2 Asking questions 5 marks

1 What was the conference like?
2 How long did the conference last?
3 What were the facilities like?
4 Were the presentations very interesting?
5 How many people attended your presentation?

3 Size and dimension 10 marks

1 height, high
2 heavy, weighs
3 width, wide
4 long, long
5 weigh, weight

4 Company history 10 marks

1 What happened in 1930?
2 When did BASF launch its famous magnetic tape?
3 What division did BASF establish in 1968?
4 Where did BASF open an environmental control centre in 1989?
5 Which anniversary did BASF celebrate in 1995?

5 Vocabulary quiz 10 marks

1 uncomfortable
2 inefficient
3 shape
4 competition
5 adjustable
6 feasibility
7 vegetables
8 biography
9 go, do

6 Saying when 10 marks

1 in
2 in
3 at
4 on
5 at
6 on
7 at
8 on
9 at
10 in

7 Spot the mistake 20 marks

1 What was your vacation like?
2 We were all very bored …
3 … you use to write on OHTs.
4 … making mistakes.
5 Where did you go …
6 When did the new system start?
7 He arrived here last Monday.
8 … some chicken/a piece of chicken, please.
9 … once a week.
10 What does 'selective' mean?

8 Social English   10 marks

1 f
2 a
3 e
4 h
5 j
6 g
7 d
8 i
9 c
10 b

9 Past developments   15 marks

launched, set up, was, became, thought, established, got, grew, developed, linked, created, were, rose, transferred, had

TEST 3

1 A meeting   10 marks

We need to discuss, think we should, do you feel, I disagree, do you think, I don't think, Why don't, Shall we, That's a good idea, be responsible for this

2 Giving reasons   5 marks

1 am going to
2 isn't going to
3 are going to
4 am not going to
5 aren't going to

3 Plans and arrangements   5 marks

1 When are you seeing Peter?
2 What time does the conference begin?
3 Is he arriving tomorrow morning?
4 When does the next plane to London leave?
5 When are you going to start your new job?

4 Arrangements   20 marks

1 It leaves at 7.40 on Tuesday.
2 It begins at 9.30 am.
3 She's meeting him at 1.30 pm on Tuesday.
4 She's having dinner with Christian and Uli.
5 She's going to (the) Head Office.
6 When/What time does she arrive in Frankfurt?
7 Where's she having dinner/ What's she doing on Tuesday evening?
8 When/What time is she giving her presentation?
9 When is she flying to London/home?
10 When/What time does her flight arrive in London?

5 Invitations   10 marks

1 What are you doing on Friday evening?
2 Nothing special. Why?
3 I'm meeting Jo for dinner. How about joining us?
4 That's a good idea. Where are you going?
5 Michel's Restaurant. Do you know it?
6 No. Where is it?
7 In the city centre. Opposite the station.
8 Oh, I know the place. What time?
9 8 o'clock.
10 Great. See you there, then.

6 Making appointments   10 marks

free, afraid, tied, How/What, good/convenient, manage/make, fine/OK, forward, seeing/meeting, then

7 Spot the mistake   20 marks

1 We should leave …
2 Why don't we …
3 Why are they …
4 When does your flight leave?
5 … increased by 7%.
6 How about coming …
7 'I agree.'
8 I don't think …
9 Tim didn't agree …
10 Would you like to go …

8 Trends   10 marks

1 fell sharply
2 recovered slightly
3 from, to
4 went, by
5 remained steady, at
6 rose
7 of

9 Vocabulary quiz   10 marks

1 borrowed
2 by
3 on
4 dramatically
5 due to
6 in
7 figures
8 postpone
9 steady
10 fell

TEST 4

1 Recent achievements   10 marks

has achieved, has become, has been, have increased, has built, have grown, have shown, have risen, has resulted, have fallen

2 Performance   5 marks

1 Have you improved your sales performance?
2 Which division has achieved the best results?
3 Has your division exceeded its target?
4 Have all the divisions achieved their targets?
5 How much has your turnover increased this year?

3 Checking progress   15 marks

1 Have you checked the flight yet? Yes, I have.
2 Have you booked a/your/my ticket (to Paris) yet? Yes, I have.
3 Have you rung Pete Burns yet? No, I haven't.
4 Have you arranged a meeting with Donald yet? Yes, I have, for 10.30 on Friday.
5 Have you written a/the (sales) report yet? No, I haven't.

4 Quantity   10 marks

1 much
2 many
3 much
4 many
5 many
6 much
7 much
8 many
9 much
10 many

5 Giving advice   **5 marks**

1b 2e 3d 4c 5a

6 Predictions   **5 marks**

1 Unemployment won't go up in Denmark.
2 Unemployment won't fall in France.
3 Unemployment will rise in Norway.
4 Unemployment will remain steady in Spain.
5 Unemployment won't decrease in Switzerland.

7 Comparisons   **20 marks**

more convenient, longer, better, the most popular, the most expensive, cheaper, more expensive, the cheapest, the most reliable, the best.

8 Spot the mistake   **20 marks**

1 … we have been very busy.
2 We have achieved all our sales targets this year./ We achieved all our sales targets last year.
3 … some information.
4 … much time.
5 … when I see him.
6 You'd better not go …
7 Shall I help you?
8 We expect to increase …
9 … are cheaper …
10 … the most expensive.

9 Vocabulary quiz   **10 marks**

1 target
2 stockbroker
3 dividend
4 retirement
5 resign
6 inflation
7 shortage
8 redundant
9 margin
10 recruit

TEST 5

1 Company rules   **10 marks**

1 mustn't
2 must, don't have to, mustn't, don't have to
3 must, must, mustn't
4 mustn't
5 don't have to

2 If …   **10 marks**

1 f
2 h
3 b
4 i
5 e
6 c
7 j
8 a
9 g
10 d

3 Possibilities   **10 marks**

1 drop, will damage
2 hear, will tell
3 see
4 don't finish, will miss
5 open
6 will give, rings

4 How long   **10 marks**

1 since
2 for
3 for
4 since
5 for
6 since
7 for
8 since
9 since
10 for

5 Career history   **10 marks**

1 has she been
2 did she become
3 did she work
4 has she worked
5 did she join
6 has she worked
7 did she live
8 did she move
9 has she had
10 has she changed

6 Experiences   **10 marks**

1 I've never broken, I broke
2 has been learning, hasn't passed
3 I've worked, I haven't worked
4 Have you ever used, have
5 have had to, haven't given

7 Safety procedure   **10 marks**

is discovered, is sounded, are closed, are required, is contacted, are requested, are told, are conducted, are obliged, are kept

8 Spot the mistake   **20 marks**

1 If you have a problem …
2 … I can't leave yet.
3 … for three weeks.
4 Tim never went/has never been to Africa.
5 What time did you arrive
6 I have been working …
7 Where are Swatch watches manufactured?
8 The circuit boards are assembled …
9 … to do my homework.
10 If you leave now …

9 Vocabulary quiz   **10 marks**

1 overbooked
2 economy
3 advance
4 public
5 inventory
6 custom
7 refund
8 discount
9 overheads
10 extend